Mastering Your Money

A Comprehensive Guide to Personal Finance

Mastering Your Money: A Comprehensive Guide to Personal Finance

Contents

Mastering Your Money: A Comprehensive Guide to Personal Finance

I. Introduction

A. The Importance of Personal Finance

Personal finance is a fundamental aspect of our lives, impacting our ability to achieve our goals, provide for our families, and secure our financial future. In this introductory section, we will explore the significance of personal finance, set the stage for your financial journey, and provide an overview of the key concepts and principles that will be covered in this comprehensive guide.

Personal finance encompasses all the decisions and activities related to managing your money, from budgeting and saving to investing and retirement planning. It plays a pivotal role in your overall well-being and can significantly impact the quality of your life. Here's why personal finance matters:

1. **Financial Freedom:** Effective personal finance empowers you to attain financial freedom, giving you the ability to make choices based on your goals and desires rather than financial constraints.
2. **Security and Peace of Mind:** It provides a safety net for unexpected expenses and emergencies, reducing financial stress and anxiety.
3. **Wealth Building:** Personal finance strategies help you build wealth over time, ensuring financial stability in the present and a comfortable retirement in the future.

4. **Achievement of Goals:** Whether it's buying a home, funding your children's education, or traveling the world, personal finance is the means to achieve your aspirations.

B. Setting Financial Goals

Before diving into the specifics of managing your finances, it's essential to define your financial goals. Your goals serve as the North Star, guiding your financial decisions and actions. They can be short-term (e.g., paying off credit card debt), mid-term (e.g., buying a car), or long-term (e.g., retiring comfortably).

Setting clear and achievable financial goals is a crucial step in your personal finance journey. Here's how to do it:

1. **Define Your Goals:** Take the time to articulate your financial aspirations. What do you want to accomplish with your money? Be specific and realistic.
2. **Prioritize Your Goals:** Not all goals are equal in terms of urgency and importance. Determine which goals should take precedence based on your current life stage and circumstances.
3. **Set Measurable Targets:** Quantify your goals. For instance, if you aim to save for retirement, specify the amount you need to save each month to reach that goal.
4. **Create a Timeline:** Assign a timeframe to each goal. This adds a sense of urgency and helps you track your progress.

5. **Review and Adjust:** Periodically revisit your goals to ensure they remain relevant. Life circumstances can change, and your goals may need to evolve accordingly.

C. Overview of the Book's Content

In the chapters that follow, we will delve into various aspects of personal finance, equipping you with the knowledge and tools to make informed financial decisions. Here's a sneak peek at what you can expect:

- **Building a Strong Financial Foundation:** We'll explore budgeting basics, managing debt, and the importance of emergency funds to lay a solid financial groundwork.
- **Saving and Investing:** Learn how to save for short-term goals and invest for long-term wealth. We'll cover investment options, risk tolerance, and retirement planning.
- **Income Generation:** Maximize your earning potential through career development and explore strategies for effective tax planning.
- **Protecting Your Finances:** Understand the importance of insurance, estate planning, and how to secure your financial future.

- **Financial Milestones:** Navigate significant life events like buying a home, getting married, and planning for retirement.
- **Navigating Financial Challenges:** Learn how to handle financial setbacks and stress effectively.
- **Advanced Financial Strategies:** Explore advanced concepts such as investment diversification, tax optimization, and charitable giving.
- **Staying Informed and Adapting:** Discover how to stay updated on financial news and adapt your financial strategies as life evolves.

This guide will empower you to take control of your financial future, make wise financial decisions, and achieve the financial well-being and security you deserve. As we embark on this journey together, remember that personal finance is not a one-size-fits-all endeavor. Your financial path is unique, and this guide is here to provide the knowledge and tools you need to navigate it successfully.

II. Building a Strong Financial Foundation

A. Budgeting Basics

Here we dive deep into the core principles of budgeting, providing readers with a solid foundation for managing their personal finances effectively. At its heart, budgeting is the art of creating a financial roadmap that helps individuals take control of their spending, allocate resources wisely, and work towards their financial goals.

This chapter begins by emphasizing the paramount importance of budgeting. Just as a ship needs a captain and a map, your financial journey requires a budget to steer you in the right direction. By tracking income and expenses, readers will gain a clear understanding of where their money goes, empowering them to make informed financial choices.

Readers will learn how to create a budget step by step, starting with calculating their income from various sources. They'll then explore different expense categories, differentiating between fixed expenses (like rent or mortgage payments and utilities) and variable expenses (such as groceries, entertainment, and dining out). Armed with this knowledge, readers can allocate their income to these categories while taking their financial goals into account. Additionally, the chapter provides insights into the importance of maintaining an emergency fund, which acts as a financial safety net, ensuring that unexpected expenses or emergencies don't derail your financial journey. By the end of the chapter, readers will have a clear understanding of how to create and manage a budget, a skill that is essential for financial success.

Budgeting is the cornerstone of sound financial management. In this chapter, we embark on a journey into the heart of personal finance, delving into the fundamental principles of budgeting that are essential for taking control of your financial life.

At its core, a budget is a powerful tool that helps you keep track of your income and expenses. It's more than just a spreadsheet or a list of numbers; it's your financial roadmap, guiding you towards your goals and ensuring that your financial decisions align with your priorities.

Budgeting is the cornerstone of sound financial management. It serves as a roadmap for your money, ensuring that you allocate funds to meet your needs, wants, and financial goals. In this section, we'll delve into the fundamentals of budgeting, guiding you through the process of creating a budget that empowers you to take control of your finances.

Budgeting is not merely about restricting your spending; it's about empowerment and financial clarity. Here's why budgeting is so important:

Financial Awareness: A budget provides a clear picture of your financial situation. It allows you to see where your money is coming from and where it's going, which is the first step toward informed decision-making.

Goal Achievement: Budgeting helps you allocate funds to your financial goals. Whether you're saving for a vacation, paying off debt, or building an emergency fund, a budget ensures that you make progress toward these objectives.

Control and Discipline: With a budget, you are in control of your finances rather than letting your finances control you. It encourages disciplined spending and prevents you from overspending in any particular category.

Financial Stability: Budgeting helps you avoid financial surprises. By accounting for regular expenses and saving for emergencies, you create a safety net that provides stability and peace of mind.

Imagine setting out on a road trip without a map or GPS. You might end up lost, disoriented, and unsure of where you're headed. Similarly, managing your finances without a budget can lead to financial disarray. Budgeting provides the much-needed roadmap for your financial journey, allowing you to navigate life's twists and turns with confidence.

At its core, budgeting helps you answer vital financial questions:

Where is your money going? Tracking your expenses reveals where your hard-earned cash is actually spent. This awareness is the first step towards making informed financial decisions.

Are you living within your means? A budget helps you compare your income to your expenditures. If you're consistently spending more than you earn, it's a red flag that you need to make adjustments.

Can you save or invest for the future? Budgeting carves out a portion of your income for saving and investing, ensuring you build wealth over time and achieve your financial goals.

1. Creating a Budget

Creating a budget might seem daunting at first, but it's a straightforward process once you break it down into steps:

1. **Calculate Your Income:** Begin by determining your total monthly income. This includes your salary, any side hustle earnings, rental income, or other sources of cash flow.
2. **List Your Expenses:** Next, catalog all your monthly expenses. These can be categorized into fixed expenses (e.g., rent or mortgage, utilities, insurance) and variable expenses (e.g., groceries, entertainment, dining out).
3. **Identify Your Financial Goals:** Reflect on your short-term and long-term financial goals. These might include building an emergency fund, paying off debt, or saving for a vacation or retirement.

4. **Allocate Funds:** Allocate a portion of your income to each expense category while keeping your financial goals in mind. Be realistic about your spending habits and prioritize essential expenses.
5. **Track and Adjust:** After creating your budget, it's crucial to track your actual spending. Use tools like spreadsheets or budgeting apps to monitor how your expenses align with your budget. If you overspend in one category, adjust accordingly in another to stay on track.

2. Tracking Expenses

Within the realm of budgeting basics, tracking expenses is a fundamental practice that provides invaluable insights into your financial habits and lays the groundwork for responsible financial management. In this section, we explore the crucial task of monitoring and categorizing your expenditures, shedding light on where your money is truly going and empowering you to make informed financial decisions.

Tracking expenses is akin to shining a spotlight on your financial life. It brings clarity to your spending patterns, helping you identify areas where you can cut back, save more, or reallocate resources towards your financial goals. This process can be eye-opening, as many people are surprised to discover how seemingly small, regular expenses can add up over time.

To get started with tracking expenses, begin by recording every purchase, no matter how minor, for a designated period, such as a month. Use a notebook, smartphone app, or spreadsheet to categorize each expense, grouping them into fixed (predictable, regular expenses like rent or mortgage, utilities, and insurance) and variable (fluctuating, discretionary expenses like dining out, entertainment, and shopping) categories. This exercise not only reveals your spending habits but also highlights opportunities for saving and reallocating funds towards more meaningful financial objectives.

This chapter will help you not only understand the importance of tracking expenses but also possess the tools and knowledge needed to implement this essential practice effectively. It's a crucial step on your journey to mastering your money and achieving financial well-being.

Tracking expenses is the meticulous art of monitoring every financial transaction, no matter how minor, with the goal of gaining complete visibility into your spending patterns. In Chapter II.A.2, we delve into the significance of this practice and provide practical guidance on how to implement it effectively.

One of the most compelling reasons to track expenses is to uncover where your money truly goes. It's astonishing how the seemingly insignificant daily expenditures, like morning coffee or dining out for lunch, can add up over time. Tracking expenses reveals these financial leaks and empowers you to make conscious decisions about your spending.

We introduce you to various methods for tracking expenses, ranging from traditional pen-and-paper tracking to utilizing budgeting apps and software. Regardless of the method chosen, the primary goal is to categorize expenses into fixed and variable categories. Fixed expenses encompass regular, predictable payments like rent or mortgage, utilities, and insurance. On the other hand, variable expenses consist of discretionary spending on things like dining out, entertainment, and non-essential shopping.

There are various tools available for tracking expenses, ranging from traditional methods to modern digital solutions. Here are some popular tools and approaches for tracking expenses:

1. **Pen and Paper:** The simplest method is to keep a physical ledger or notebook where you record all your expenses manually. This method is low-tech but can be effective for those who prefer a tangible record.
2. **Excel or Google Sheets:** Spreadsheets are versatile and customizable tools for expense tracking. You can create your expense categories, input data, and use formulas for automatic calculations. Google Sheets allows for cloud-based collaboration and access from multiple devices.

3. **Envelope System:** This is a cash-based budgeting method where you allocate a specific amount of cash to different spending categories and use physical envelopes to store the money. Once the envelope is empty, you've reached your spending limit for that category.

4. **Expense Tracking Apps:** Numerous apps are designed for expense tracking, such as Mint, YNAB (You Need a Budget), PocketGuard, and Personal Capital. These apps link to your bank accounts and credit cards to automatically categorize and track your expenses. They often provide insights, budgeting tools, and visualizations of your financial data.

5. **Bank and Credit Card Statements:** Most banks and credit card providers offer online access to your transaction history and statements. Reviewing these regularly can help you track your expenses, especially if your transactions are primarily digital.

6. **Receipt Scanning Apps:** Apps like Receipts by Wave or Expensify allow you to scan and digitize paper receipts. This can be particularly useful for business expenses and tax purposes.

7. **Note-Taking Apps:** If you prefer simplicity, note-taking apps like Evernote or Apple Notes can be used to jot down expenses manually. Create separate notes for different categories and update them as you spend.

8. **Manual Mobile Expense Trackers:** Some apps, like Goodbudget, enable manual entry of expenses on your mobile device. This can be useful if you prefer not to link your financial accounts directly.
9. **Photographing Receipts:** You can use your smartphone camera to take pictures of receipts, which can then be organized and categorized using note-taking or dedicated receipt-tracking apps.
10. **Credit Card and Expense Management Software:** Businesses often use specialized software like QuickBooks, FreshBooks, or Xero for expense tracking, invoice management, and financial reporting. These tools can also be beneficial for freelancers and self-employed individuals.

The choice of expense tracking tool depends on your personal preferences, comfort with technology, and the level of detail you desire in your expense tracking. Many people find that using a combination of methods, such as a mobile app for day-to-day expenses and a spreadsheet for more comprehensive budgeting, works best for them. Ultimately, the key is to select a tool that aligns with your financial goals and helps you maintain financial discipline.

By diligently tracking expenses, you'll gain insights into your spending habits, identify areas where you can cut back or optimize, and ultimately take greater control of your financial life. This practice is the cornerstone of effective budgeting, allowing you to align your spending with your financial goals and priorities. As you progress through this chapter, you'll develop the skills and discipline necessary to track your expenses routinely, setting the stage for more advanced financial management strategies in the chapters that follow.

3. Emergency Funds

Within budgeting basics, creating an emergency fund deserves special attention. An emergency fund is a financial safety net that provides peace of mind during unexpected crises, such as medical expenses, car repairs, or job loss. Financial experts typically recommend saving three to six months' worth of living expenses in your emergency fund.

Your budget is the tool that helps you systematically contribute to your emergency fund. It ensures that you prioritize saving for emergencies alongside other financial goals, making it less likely that you'll be caught off guard when life throws you a curveball.

In conclusion, budgeting is not just about tracking numbers; it's about aligning your financial choices with your life goals and values. It empowers you to make informed decisions, optimize your spending, and achieve financial stability. So far, we've laid the foundation for your financial journey by emphasizing the significance of budgeting, guiding you through its creation process, and highlighting the importance of emergency funds. In the chapters that follow, we'll delve deeper into various aspects of personal finance, equipping you with the knowledge and skills to take control of your financial future.

B. Managing Debt

Debt is a financial tool that, when managed responsibly, can help you achieve important life goals like buying a home, pursuing higher education, or starting a business. However, when left uncontrolled, debt can quickly become a heavy burden that impedes your financial progress. Chapter II.B focuses on the critical aspects of managing debt effectively, helping you understand the various types of debt, explore debt reduction strategies, and delve into the importance of credit scores and credit reports in your financial life.

1. Understanding Different Types of Debt

Debt comes in various forms, each with its own set of terms, interest rates, and implications. To manage debt effectively, it's essential to grasp the distinctions between these types:

   a. **Consumer Debt:** This category includes debts incurred for personal expenses, such as credit card balances, personal loans, and payday loans. Consumer debt often carries higher interest rates, making it more expensive to maintain over time.
   b. **Mortgage Debt:** A mortgage is a loan used to purchase real estate, typically a home. Mortgages typically have lower interest rates compared to consumer debt and can

be considered "good" debt when used for homeownership.

c. **Student Loans:** Student loans finance education expenses and come with various terms and interest rates. Federal student loans may offer more favorable terms and repayment options than private student loans.

d. **Auto Loans:** These loans are used to purchase vehicles. Like mortgages, auto loans usually have lower interest rates compared to consumer debt.

e. **Business Debt:** Entrepreneurs often take on business debt to fund their ventures. The terms and interest rates for business loans can vary widely.

f. **Medical Debt:** Medical expenses can result in debt, often due to unexpected healthcare costs. Medical providers may offer payment plans or financial assistance options.

Understanding the nature of your debt is the first step toward effective debt management. You should be aware of the interest rates, repayment terms, and any potential consequences of defaulting on these debts.

2. Debt Reduction Strategies

Managing debt isn't just about making minimum payments; it's about developing a clear strategy to reduce and eliminate your debts efficiently. Here are some debt reduction strategies to consider:

a. **Snowball Method:** With this approach, you focus on paying off the smallest debts first while making minimum payments on others. As each small debt is eliminated, you move on to the next, creating a sense of accomplishment and motivation.

b. **Avalanche Method:** This strategy prioritizes debts with the highest interest rates. By targeting high-interest debts first, you minimize the total interest paid over time.

c. **Debt Consolidation:** This involves combining multiple debts into a single loan, often with a lower interest rate. Debt consolidation can simplify payments and reduce the overall interest burden.

d. **Negotiating with Creditors:** If you're struggling to make payments, consider contacting your creditors to discuss options such as lower interest rates, extended repayment terms, or settlement agreements.

e. **Budgeting and Lifestyle Adjustments:** Review your budget to identify areas where you can cut expenses and allocate more money toward debt repayment. Making temporary lifestyle adjustments can free up additional funds for debt reduction.

f. Windfalls and Bonuses: Windfalls like tax refunds or work bonuses can provide a significant boost to your debt reduction efforts. Consider directing unexpected income toward debt payoff.

3. Credit Scores and Reports

Your credit score and credit report are vital components of your financial health. They impact your ability to access credit, secure favorable interest rates, and even influence job opportunities in some cases. Chapter II.B explores these concepts in-depth:

a. **Credit Score:** Your credit score is a numerical representation of your creditworthiness. It is typically calculated using information from your credit report. The most common credit score model is the FICO score, which ranges from 300 to 850. A higher score indicates better creditworthiness and may lead to more favorable lending terms.

b. **Credit Report:** Your credit report is a detailed record of your credit history. It includes information about your open and closed credit accounts, payment history, credit inquiries, and public records like bankruptcies. It's important to review your credit report regularly to check for errors or inaccuracies that could affect your credit score.

c. **Building and Maintaining Good Credit:** Understanding how credit scores are calculated and what factors influence them is crucial for building and maintaining good credit. This chapter provides guidance on actions you can take to improve your credit score over time, such as making on-time payments, reducing debt balances, and managing credit responsibly.

    d. **Monitoring Your Credit:** Regularly monitoring your credit score and credit report helps you stay aware of your financial standing and detect any suspicious activity or errors. You can use free annual credit reports from each of the major credit bureaus or subscribe to credit monitoring services.

Managing debt wisely is a crucial aspect of achieving financial stability and realizing your financial goals. By comprehending the various types of debt, employing effective debt reduction strategies, and proactively managing your credit score and credit report, you can take control of your financial future and work towards a debt-free life. This chapter equipped you with the knowledge and tools necessary to tackle your debts head-on and make informed decisions about your financial well-being.

III. Saving and Investing
A. Saving for Short-Term Goals

Saving for short-term goals is an essential component of financial planning. Short-term goals typically encompass objectives you aim to achieve within the next one to three years, such as a vacation, buying a new car, or covering upcoming educational expenses. What distinguishes short-term savings from long-term investments is the relatively brief time horizon, which requires a different approach.

First, identify your specific short-term goals and set clear, achievable targets. Knowing exactly what you're saving for helps maintain focus and motivation. Next, establish a separate savings account or fund dedicated exclusively to these goals. This separation ensures that the money earmarked for short-term objectives isn't mingled with funds intended for long-term investments or emergency expenses.

Once your savings account is in place, create a realistic savings plan by determining how much you need to save each month to reach your short-term goal within the desired timeframe. This plan should be based on your current financial situation and budget. Automating regular contributions to your short-term savings account can make the process effortless and help you stay on track. Additionally, consider utilizing high-yield savings accounts or certificates of deposit (CDs) to earn a bit more interest on your short-term savings while keeping them easily accessible when you need them. Short-term saving not only allows you to enjoy life's pleasures and fulfill immediate aspirations but also builds a strong foundation for responsible financial management.

1. Creating a Savings Plan

Creating a savings plan is a critical step in achieving your financial goals and ensuring financial security. Whether you're saving for an emergency fund, a vacation, a down payment on a home, or retirement, a well-structured savings plan provides the roadmap to reach your objectives. Here's how to create an effective savings plan:

a. **Set Clear Goals:** Start by defining your savings goals. Be specific about what you're saving for, whether it's short-term or long-term. Having clear goals will help you stay motivated and track your progress.

b. **Determine Your Timeline:** Establish a timeframe for each savings goal. Knowing when you want to achieve your objectives allows you to calculate how much you need to save each month. Short-term goals may have a one-year timeframe, while long-term goals like retirement could span several decades.

c. **Calculate the Required Savings:** Determine how much money you need to reach each goal. Break this down into monthly or weekly contributions, making it easier to incorporate into your budget.

d. **Review Your Budget:** Analyze your current income and expenses. A detailed budget will reveal how much disposable income you have available for savings. If you find that your expenses are too high to comfortably save for your goals, consider making adjustments to your spending habits.

e. **Automate Your Savings:** One of the most effective ways to stick to your savings plan is to automate your contributions. Set up automatic transfers from your checking account to your dedicated savings accounts for each goal. This ensures that you consistently save without the temptation to spend the money.

f. **Emergency Fund:** Prioritize building an emergency fund as part of your savings plan. Aim to save at least three to six months' worth of living expenses to provide a financial safety net in case of unexpected events like medical emergencies or job loss.

g. **Regularly Monitor and Adjust:** Periodically review your savings plan to track your progress and make necessary adjustments. Life circumstances and financial goals can change, so your savings plan should be flexible enough to accommodate these shifts.

Creating a savings plan not only helps you achieve your financial aspirations but also instills discipline and financial responsibility. It's a crucial step on the path to financial well-being and peace of mind.

2. High-Yield Savings Accounts

High-yield savings accounts are a valuable financial tool for individuals looking to earn a competitive interest rate on their savings while maintaining easy access to their funds. These accounts are offered by banks and credit unions and provide a more attractive interest rate compared to traditional savings accounts. Here's a closer look at the key features and benefits of high-yield savings accounts:

a. **Higher Interest Rates:** The primary draw of high-yield savings accounts is the significantly higher interest rates they offer in comparison to standard savings accounts. While traditional savings accounts typically provide minimal interest, high-yield savings accounts aim to maximize your earnings. The exact interest rate can vary among financial institutions, but it's common for high-yield savings accounts to yield rates multiple times higher than regular accounts.

b. **Liquidity and Accessibility:** High-yield savings accounts strike a balance between earning interest and maintaining liquidity. Unlike some long-term investment options, your funds remain easily accessible. You can withdraw money from a high-yield savings account without facing penalties or restrictions, making it an ideal choice for saving for short-term goals, emergency funds, or any situation where you need quick access to your money.

c. **Low Risk:** High-yield savings accounts are considered low-risk investments because they are typically insured up to a certain limit by the Federal Deposit Insurance Corporation (FDIC) for banks or the National Credit Union Administration (NCUA) for credit unions. This means that even if the financial institution experiences financial difficulties, your deposited funds, up to the insured limit, are protected.

d. **No Fees or Minimum Balance Requirements:** Many high-yield savings accounts have no monthly fees or minimum balance requirements. This ensures that you can start saving without incurring extra costs or being forced to maintain a specific balance in your account.

e. **Competitive Market:** Competition among financial institutions for customers' deposits has led to continuous improvements in the offerings of high-yield savings accounts. Banks and credit unions may offer promotional interest rates, cash bonuses for opening an account, or other incentives to attract savers.

f. **Online Access:** High-yield savings accounts are often offered by online banks, which means you can manage your account conveniently through web and mobile applications. This eliminates the need to visit physical branches and allows for 24/7 access to your account information.

While high-yield savings accounts offer numerous advantages, it's important to keep in mind that they may not provide the same level of returns as riskier investment options like stocks or bonds. These accounts are best suited for funds you want to keep safe and easily accessible, such as your emergency fund or savings for short-term goals. When considering a high-yield savings account, compare interest rates, fees, and account terms offered by different financial institutions to find the one that best aligns with your financial objectives.

B. Investing for Long-Term Wealth

Investing for long-term wealth is a fundamental strategy for achieving financial security, building wealth, and securing a comfortable retirement. This approach recognizes the power of compound interest and time as key allies in growing your financial assets. Here's a closer look at the principles and benefits of investing for long-term wealth:

1. **The Power of Compound Interest:** Long-term investing harnesses the remarkable power of compound interest. Compound interest means that not only do you earn interest on your initial investment, but you also earn interest on the interest you've already earned. Over time, this compounding effect can significantly multiply your wealth. The longer you stay invested, the more time your money has to grow exponentially.

2. **Diversification and Risk Management:** A key principle of long-term investing is diversification. By spreading your investments across different asset

classes, such as stocks, bonds, real estate, and other alternatives, you reduce the risk associated with any single investment. Diversification helps protect your portfolio during market fluctuations and economic downturns, ensuring more consistent long-term returns.

3. **Historical Market Performance:** Historical data shows that, over extended periods, financial markets tend to trend upward, despite short-term fluctuations. While markets may experience volatility and downturns, they have historically rebounded and continued to grow. Long-term investors have the advantage of weathering these ups and downs and benefiting from the overall upward trajectory of markets.

4. **Retirement Planning:** Long-term investing is especially crucial for retirement planning. As life expectancies increase, retirees need a source of income that can last several decades. Investing in assets like stocks and bonds can provide a reliable source of income and growth potential during retirement.

5. **Tax Efficiency:** Long-term investors often benefit from tax advantages. In many countries, investments held for an extended period may qualify for lower capital gains tax rates. Tax-efficient investing strategies can help you minimize your tax liability over time, allowing your investments to grow more efficiently.

6. **Passive Investing and Index Funds:** Passive investing, which involves holding a diversified portfolio of assets without frequent buying and selling, is a popular approach for long-term investors. Index funds, for example, provide exposure to a broad market index and tend to have lower fees compared to actively managed funds. This passive approach aligns with the "buy and hold" strategy that is characteristic of long-term wealth-building.

7. **Regular Contributions:** Consistently adding money to your investments through regular contributions, such as monthly or annual deposits, is another essential element of long-term wealth-building. Regular contributions help maximize the benefits of compound interest and ensure your portfolio continues to grow over time.

8. **Behavioral Discipline:** Patience and discipline are key traits of successful long-term investors. Emotional reactions to market fluctuations can lead to impulsive decisions that harm your portfolio. Staying the course and adhering to your long-term investment strategy, even in challenging times, is crucial for realizing the full potential of your investments.

Investing for long-term wealth is not a get-rich-quick scheme; it's a strategy that requires time, discipline, and a well-thought-out plan. The earlier you start, the more time your investments have to grow, making long-term investing a powerful tool for achieving your financial goals and securing your future.

1. Types of Investments (Stocks, Bonds, Real Estate, etc.)

Investing is a vital component of wealth-building and achieving your financial goals. When building an investment portfolio, diversification is key to spreading risk and optimizing returns. To accomplish this, you can invest in various asset classes, each with its own characteristics, risk profiles, and potential for returns. In this comprehensive exploration, we will delve into different types of investments, including stocks, bonds, real estate, and alternative assets.

Stocks (Equities)

Definition: Stocks represent ownership shares in a publicly traded company. When you own stocks, you own a portion of the company and have the potential to share in its profits through capital appreciation and dividends.

Key Points:

- **Capital Appreciation:** Stocks have the potential for significant capital appreciation, meaning their value can increase over time. This makes them a popular choice for long-term investors.

- **Dividends:** Some companies pay dividends to their shareholders, providing a source of income. Dividend stocks are favored by income-oriented investors.

- **Risk:** Stocks can be volatile, with prices subject to market fluctuations. Diversification and a long-term perspective can help mitigate this risk.

- **Types:** Stocks come in various types, including common stocks, preferred stocks, and different classes of shares. Common stocks grant voting rights in the company, while preferred stocks offer priority in dividend payments.

Who Should Invest: Stocks are suitable for investors seeking long-term growth and willing to accept higher volatility in exchange for potentially higher returns.

Bonds (Fixed-Income Securities)

Definition: Bonds are debt securities issued by governments, municipalities, corporations, or other entities. When you buy a bond, you're essentially lending money to the issuer in exchange for periodic interest payments (coupon) and the return of the bond's face value (principal) at maturity.

Key Points:

- **Stability:** Bonds are generally considered less risky than stocks and provide a stable source of income through regular interest payments.

- **Maturity:** Bonds have set maturity dates, ranging from short-term (e.g., one year) to long-term (e.g., 30 years).

The longer the maturity, the higher the interest rate investors typically receive.

- **Credit Risk:** Bond investments come with credit risk, meaning the issuer may default on interest payments or fail to repay the principal. Credit rating agencies assess and assign credit ratings to bonds to help investors gauge risk.

- **Types:** Bonds include government bonds, municipal bonds, corporate bonds, and Treasury bonds (U.S. government bonds).

Who Should Invest: Bonds are suitable for income-focused investors, retirees, or those looking to balance the risk in their portfolio with more stable assets.

Real Estate

Definition: Real estate investments involve purchasing physical properties or indirect ownership through real estate investment trusts (REITs). Real estate can encompass residential, commercial, industrial, and agricultural properties.

Key Points:

- **Income and Appreciation:** Real estate investments offer potential rental income and property appreciation. Rental income provides a consistent cash flow, while property values may increase over time.

- **Diversification:** Real estate can diversify a portfolio by providing an asset class with a low correlation to stocks and bonds. This can enhance risk management.

- **Liquidity:** Real estate investments can be less liquid than stocks and bonds, as it may take time to buy or sell properties.

- **Types:** Real estate investments include physical properties, REITs (publicly traded companies that own and manage real estate portfolios), and real estate partnerships.

Who Should Invest: Real estate is suitable for investors looking for income, diversification, and potential long-term appreciation in their portfolio.

Mutual Funds and Exchange-Traded Funds (ETFs)

Definition: Mutual funds and ETFs are investment vehicles that pool money from multiple investors to purchase a diversified portfolio of stocks, bonds, or other assets. They offer diversification without requiring investors to directly buy individual securities.

Key Points:

- **Diversification:** Mutual funds and ETFs provide instant diversification by holding a basket of assets.

This reduces risk associated with individual stock or bond selection.

- **Professional Management:** These funds are managed by professional portfolio managers who make investment decisions on behalf of investors.

- **Liquidity:** Mutual funds and ETFs are highly liquid, allowing investors to buy or sell shares on any trading day at market prices.

- **Types:** There are various types of mutual funds and ETFs, including equity funds, bond funds, sector-specific funds, and thematic ETFs.

Who Should Invest: Mutual funds and ETFs are suitable for investors seeking diversification, professional management, and easy liquidity in their investments.

Alternative Investments

Definition: Alternative investments cover a broad spectrum of assets beyond traditional stocks and bonds. These can include commodities, precious metals, hedge funds, private equity, venture capital, and even cryptocurrencies like Bitcoin.

Key Points:

- **Diversification:** Alternative investments offer further diversification by introducing assets with unique risk-return profiles that may not correlate closely with traditional investments.

- **Risk and Complexity:** Many alternative investments come with higher risk and complexity, requiring thorough research and understanding before investing.

- **Illiquidity:** Some alternative investments, like private equity or real estate partnerships, may have longer investment horizons and limited liquidity.

- **Potential High Returns:** Alternative investments can offer the potential for high returns, making them attractive to investors seeking opportunities beyond traditional markets.

Who Should Invest: Alternative investments are suitable for sophisticated investors willing to conduct in-depth research and manage the complexities and risks associated with these assets.

Conclusion

Diversifying your investment portfolio by incorporating various asset classes can help manage risk and optimize returns over the long term. The selection of specific investments should align with your financial goals, risk tolerance, and investment horizon. Keep in mind that building a well-balanced portfolio often involves a mix of these different types of investments to achieve your financial objectives while managing risk effectively.

2. Risk Tolerance and Asset Allocation

When it comes to investing, two fundamental concepts play a pivotal role in determining your financial success: risk tolerance and asset allocation. These factors guide your investment decisions and help you build a resilient portfolio that aligns with your financial goals and comfort level. Let's explore these concepts in detail.

Risk Tolerance: What Is It?

Risk tolerance refers to your ability and willingness to endure the inherent fluctuations and uncertainties of financial markets. It's a personal and subjective measure that varies from one investor to another. Understanding your risk tolerance is crucial because it influences the types of investments you choose and how you allocate your assets.

Several factors can influence your risk tolerance:

1. **Financial Goals:** Your specific financial objectives play a significant role. For instance, saving for retirement might allow for a longer investment horizon and a higher tolerance for risk, while saving for a short-term goal, like buying a home, might require a more conservative approach.

2. **Time Horizon:** The length of time you plan to invest can impact your risk tolerance. Generally, longer time horizons provide more opportunities to recover from

market downturns, which may lead to a higher risk tolerance.

3. **Financial Situation:** Your current financial situation, including your income, expenses, and overall net worth, can affect your risk tolerance. Those with substantial financial resources may have a higher tolerance for risk.

4. **Emotional Comfort:** Your emotional response to market volatility is a critical factor. If you find it challenging to stay calm during market turbulence or are prone to making impulsive decisions, you may have a lower risk tolerance.

5. **Experience and Knowledge:** Investors with a deep understanding of financial markets and investment strategies may be more comfortable taking on higher levels of risk.

Understanding your risk tolerance involves self-assessment and may require the guidance of a financial advisor. Once you have a clear sense of your risk tolerance, you can proceed to the next step: asset allocation.

Asset Allocation: The Art of Balancing Risk and Reward

Asset allocation is the process of spreading your investment capital across different asset classes, such as stocks, bonds, real estate, and cash equivalents, to achieve your financial goals while managing risk. This strategy is based on the principle that different asset classes have varying levels of risk and return potential.

Here's how asset allocation works:

1. **Diversification:** By holding a mix of asset classes in your portfolio, you reduce the risk associated with any single investment. If one asset class underperforms, the others may help offset losses.

2. **Balancing Risk:** Asset allocation allows you to align your investment portfolio with your risk tolerance. For example, if you have a high risk tolerance, you may allocate a larger portion of your portfolio to stocks, which have the potential for higher returns but also higher volatility.

3. **Risk-Return Tradeoff:** Asset allocation helps you strike a balance between risk and reward. Historically, stocks have offered higher potential returns but come with higher risk, while bonds are generally more conservative with lower expected returns.

4. **Adaptability:** As your financial goals, risk tolerance, and market conditions change, you can adjust your asset allocation to maintain a suitable risk-reward profile.

Common asset classes used in asset allocation include:

- **Stocks (Equities):** Equities offer the potential for long-term capital appreciation but come with higher volatility. They are often a core component of growth-oriented portfolios.

- **Bonds (Fixed-Income):** Bonds provide stable income through periodic interest payments and are generally considered lower risk than stocks. They are often included in income-focused portfolios.

- **Real Estate:** Real estate investments offer potential rental income and property appreciation. They can provide diversification and income for investors.

- **Cash Equivalents:** Cash equivalents, such as money market funds, provide liquidity and stability but typically offer lower returns.

- **Alternative Investments:** Alternative assets, like commodities, hedge funds, or private equity, may be included for further diversification and potential return enhancement.

The specific allocation of assets in your portfolio should align with your risk tolerance and financial goals. For example, a conservative investor with a low risk tolerance may have a portfolio consisting of a higher percentage of bonds and cash equivalents, while an aggressive investor with a high risk tolerance may have a portfolio with a larger allocation to stocks.

Conclusion

Risk tolerance and asset allocation are integral aspects of successful investing. By understanding your risk tolerance and strategically allocating your assets across various classes, you can build a well-balanced and resilient investment portfolio that not only aligns with your financial goals but also helps you navigate the ups and downs of financial markets with confidence. Regularly reviewing and adjusting your portfolio's asset allocation is essential as your financial circumstances and objectives evolve over time.

3. Retirement Planning

Retirement is a significant life event that marks the transition from a career-driven phase to a well-earned period of leisure and relaxation. To ensure a comfortable and financially secure retirement, effective retirement planning is essential. This comprehensive strategy encompasses saving, investing, and making informed decisions to create a nest egg that will support your desired lifestyle during retirement.

Why Retirement Planning Matters

1. **Longevity:** People are living longer than ever before, which means retirement can last 20 years or more.

Adequate planning is necessary to ensure your financial resources don't run out during this extended period.

2. **Declining Pension Availability:** Traditional defined benefit pension plans are becoming less common, shifting the responsibility for retirement funding to individuals. Retirement planning becomes more critical as reliance on pensions decreases.

3. **Inflation:** Inflation erodes the purchasing power of money over time. Retirement planning accounts for inflation to ensure your savings maintain their value.

4. **Maintaining Lifestyle:** Retirement planning helps you determine how to sustain your desired lifestyle during retirement. It involves estimating future expenses and matching them with income sources.

Key Components of Retirement Planning

1. **Setting Retirement Goals:** Begin by defining your retirement goals. Consider your desired retirement age, lifestyle, travel plans, and any specific activities or hobbies you wish to pursue. These goals will guide your savings and investment strategy.

2. **Creating a Retirement Budget:** Develop a detailed retirement budget that outlines your expected expenses during retirement. Include essentials like housing,

healthcare, and food, as well as discretionary spending on travel, hobbies, and entertainment.

3. **Assessing Current Savings:** Take stock of your current retirement savings, including 401(k) or 403(b) accounts, IRAs, and other investments. Determine whether you are on track to meet your retirement goals or if you need to adjust your savings rate.

4. **Saving for Retirement:** Consistently contribute to retirement accounts and other investment vehicles. Take advantage of employer-sponsored retirement plans and consider additional savings options like IRAs and brokerage accounts. The earlier you start, the more time your investments have to grow.

5. **Investment Strategy:** Develop an investment strategy that aligns with your risk tolerance and time horizon. Diversify your portfolio across different asset classes to balance risk and return potential.

6. **Understanding Social Security:** Familiarize yourself with the Social Security system. Understand when you become eligible for benefits, how benefits are calculated, and the impact of early or delayed claiming.

7. **Healthcare Planning:** Healthcare costs can be a significant expense during retirement. Consider purchasing supplemental health insurance and

exploring options like Medicare and long-term care insurance.

8. **Debt Management:** Work towards reducing or eliminating high-interest debt before retirement. Debt can eat into your retirement income and limit your financial flexibility.

9. **Estate Planning:** Estate planning involves preparing for the distribution of your assets after you pass away. It includes creating a will, designating beneficiaries, and considering strategies to minimize estate taxes.

10. **Regular Assessments:** Periodically review your retirement plan to ensure it remains on track. Adjust your contributions and investment strategy as needed to account for changes in your financial situation or goals.

Common Retirement Income Sources

1. **Personal Savings and Investments:** Your own savings and investments, including retirement accounts, can provide a substantial portion of your retirement income.

2. **Social Security:** Social Security benefits provide a reliable source of income for many retirees. The timing of when you claim benefits can impact the amount you receive.

3. **Employer Pensions:** Some employers offer pensions that provide a steady stream of income during retirement. These pensions may be defined benefit plans, defined contribution plans, or a combination of both.

4. **Part-Time Work:** Many retirees choose to work part-time during retirement to supplement their income and stay active.

5. **Annuities:** Annuities are financial products that provide a series of payments in exchange for a lump sum or periodic contributions. They can offer a guaranteed income stream during retirement.

6. **Rental Income:** If you own rental properties, the rental income can contribute to your retirement income.

7. **Inheritance:** Inheritances or windfalls can also boost your retirement income.

Conclusion

Retirement planning is a proactive and ongoing process that empowers you to enjoy a fulfilling and financially secure retirement. By setting clear goals, saving consistently, managing investments wisely, and understanding your income sources, you can build a retirement plan that aligns with your vision for the future. Start early, stay informed, and adapt your plan as needed to ensure a comfortable and worry-free retirement.

IV. Income Generation

Income generation is the process of creating various streams of revenue to support one's financial needs and goals. It goes beyond traditional employment income and involves diversifying income sources to achieve financial security and independence. There are several methods for income generation, each with its advantages and considerations.

One common approach to income generation is through employment or self-employment. This involves working for an employer, running a business, or providing freelance services to earn a salary or fees. While employment offers a steady income, self-employment can provide greater control over earnings and potentially higher income but may also entail more risk and uncertainty.

Another strategy is income generation through investments. This includes earning dividends from stocks, interest from bonds, rental income from real estate properties, or capital gains from selling investments. Investment income can be an effective way to build wealth over time and create passive income streams, but it often requires careful financial planning, risk management, and a long-term perspective. Diversifying income sources, such as combining earned income with investment income, can provide financial resilience and enhance overall income generation strategies.

A. Maximizing Your Earning Potential

Maximizing your earning potential is a proactive and strategic approach to increase your income over time. To achieve this, it's essential to continually invest in your skills and education, seek opportunities for career advancement or entrepreneurship, and negotiate for competitive compensation. Staying current with industry trends, networking, and expanding your professional network can open doors to higher-paying positions or ventures. Additionally, managing your finances wisely, such as budgeting and saving, can free up resources that can be reinvested in income-generating activities, further propelling your financial growth. Ultimately, the key to maximizing your earning potential is a combination of ongoing self-improvement, seizing opportunities, and making informed financial decisions.

1. Career Development

Career development is a lifelong journey of personal and professional growth, aimed at achieving your career goals and aspirations. It involves continuous learning, skill-building, and strategic planning to advance your career trajectory. Effective career development often includes setting clear objectives, identifying opportunities for skill enhancement, seeking mentorship or guidance, and actively networking within your industry. Whether it's pursuing promotions, exploring new career paths, or starting your own business, career development is about making deliberate choices that align with your interests, values, and long-term vision. It's a dynamic process that empowers individuals to adapt to changing workplace demands and seize opportunities for personal and professional fulfillment.

2. Side Hustles and Passive Income

In today's dynamic and interconnected world, side hustles and passive income have emerged as powerful financial strategies that allow individuals to augment their earnings and build financial stability beyond traditional employment. These two concepts represent different approaches to generating extra income, each with its own advantages and considerations.

Side Hustles

Side hustles are additional income-generating activities pursued alongside a primary job or main source of income. These ventures can take various forms, such as freelancing, consulting, online businesses, or part-time jobs. The appeal of side hustles lies in their potential to boost earnings, pay off debt, or save for specific financial goals. They also offer opportunities to explore personal passions and talents, turning hobbies or interests into profitable ventures. However, side hustles often require dedicated time and effort, and finding the right work-life balance can be a challenge. Success in side hustles relies on effective time management, market research, and marketing efforts.

Passive Income

Passive income, on the other hand, involves earning money with minimal ongoing effort or active involvement. It's the dream of making money while you sleep. Common sources of passive income include investments, rental properties, royalties, and dividends from stocks. The advantage of passive income is that it can provide financial security and independence over time, freeing you from the constraints of a traditional 9-to-5 job. However, building a substantial passive income stream typically requires significant initial capital, expertise in investment, and patience, as it may take time to see substantial returns. Passive income allows for more flexibility and time for other pursuits, making it an appealing option for those seeking financial freedom.

The Synergy

While side hustles and passive income are distinct strategies, they are not mutually exclusive. In fact, they can complement each other synergistically. A side hustle can provide the extra income needed to fund investments or create assets that generate passive income. For instance, a side hustle might generate savings that can be invested in dividend-paying stocks, creating a source of ongoing passive income. By combining both approaches, individuals can accelerate their financial goals and achieve a greater level of financial security and independence.

In an era of economic uncertainty and changing work dynamics, side hustles and passive income offer individuals the opportunity to take control of their financial futures. Whether you're looking to achieve specific short-term goals or build a sustainable long-term financial strategy, exploring these avenues can help you unlock new possibilities and enhance your financial well-being.

B. Tax Planning

Tax planning is a vital component of personal finance that plays a significant role in shaping your financial well-being. It involves understanding taxation and implementing tax-efficient strategies to optimize your financial situation while staying within the bounds of tax laws. In this comprehensive exploration of tax planning, we'll delve into the fundamentals of taxation, various types of taxes, and essential tax-efficient strategies that can help you minimize your tax liability and maximize your financial success.

1. Understanding Taxation

Taxation is the process by which governments collect revenue to fund public services and functions. Taxes are levied on various aspects of financial transactions, income, property, and consumption. Understanding the basics of taxation is crucial for effective tax planning:

Types of Taxes

a. **Income Tax:** Income tax is imposed on your earnings, including wages, salaries, business income, and investment income. The amount you owe is calculated based on your taxable income and the tax rate applicable to your income bracket.

b. **Capital Gains Tax:** Capital gains tax is levied on the profit you make from selling an asset, such as stocks, real estate, or investments. The tax rate may vary based on the duration of the investment (short-term or long-term).

c. **Property Tax:** Property tax is assessed on the value of real estate or other properties you own. It's typically paid to local governments and is used to fund local services and infrastructure.

d. **Sales Tax:** Sales tax is added to the purchase price of goods and services at the point of sale. The rate may vary by location, and certain items may be exempt from sales tax.

e. **Estate Tax and Inheritance Tax:** These taxes are imposed on the transfer of wealth from one generation to the next. They apply to the estate of the deceased or the recipient of the inheritance.

Tax Deductions and Credits

Tax deductions and credits are valuable tools for reducing your taxable income and overall tax liability. Deductions, such as those for mortgage interest, student loan interest, and charitable contributions, lower your taxable income. Tax credits, such as the Child Tax Credit or the Earned Income Tax Credit, directly reduce the amount of tax you owe.

Tax Filing Status

Your tax filing status, such as single, married filing jointly, or head of household, can significantly affect your tax liability. It determines your tax brackets and eligibility for certain deductions and credits.

Tax Planning vs. Tax Evasion

It's essential to distinguish between legitimate tax planning and illegal tax evasion. Tax planning involves using legal strategies to minimize your tax liability within the framework of tax laws. Tax evasion, on the other hand, involves deliberately misrepresenting financial information or engaging in illegal activities to evade taxes, which can lead to severe legal consequences.

2. Tax-Efficient Strategies

Tax planning aims to optimize your tax situation while staying compliant with tax laws. Here are some essential tax-efficient strategies to consider:

a. **Tax-Deferred Retirement Accounts:** Contributing to tax-deferred retirement accounts like 401(k)s or IRAs can reduce your taxable income in the current year, allowing your investments to grow tax-free until retirement. Additionally, some contributions may be tax-deductible, further reducing your tax liability.

b. **Tax-Efficient Investment Portfolios:** Constructing a tax-efficient investment portfolio can help minimize capital gains tax. Strategies like tax-loss harvesting and investing in tax-efficient funds can help reduce the tax impact of your investments.

c. **Use of Tax Credits:** Identify and utilize tax credits for which you qualify. For example, the American Opportunity Credit and Lifetime Learning Credit can help offset the cost of education expenses, while the Child Tax Credit can reduce the tax burden for families with children.

d. **Charitable Giving:** Donating to qualified charitable organizations not only benefits the causes you support but can also lead to valuable tax deductions. Keep records of your donations and claim them on your tax return.

e. **Estate Planning:** Effective estate planning can help minimize estate taxes and ensure a smooth transfer of assets to your heirs. Strategies such as gifting, trusts, and the use of the estate tax exemption can be essential components of an estate plan.

f. **Tax-Efficient Withdrawal Strategies:** In retirement, plan your withdrawals from various accounts strategically to optimize tax efficiency. Consider factors such as required minimum distributions (RMDs) from retirement accounts and the tax implications of different income sources.

g. **Tax-Advantaged Savings Accounts:** Take advantage of tax-advantaged savings accounts like Health Savings Accounts (HSAs) and Flexible Spending Accounts (FSAs) to cover qualified medical expenses and childcare costs with pre-tax dollars.

h. **Educational Savings Plans:** 529 plans and Coverdell Education Savings Accounts offer tax advantages when saving for education expenses. Earnings in these accounts grow tax-free when used for qualified education expenses.

i. **Consult a Tax Professional:** Tax laws are complex and subject to change. Seeking guidance from a qualified tax professional can ensure you're aware of all available deductions and credits, and that your tax planning aligns with current regulations.

Tax planning is an ongoing process that should adapt to your changing financial situation and goals. By staying informed about tax laws, leveraging tax-efficient strategies, and making well-informed financial decisions, you can effectively minimize your tax liability and keep more of your hard-earned money. Remember that tax planning is a critical component of your overall financial plan, contributing to your long-term financial well-being and security.

V. Protecting Your Finances

Protecting your finances is paramount to securing your financial well-being and achieving your long-term goals. This entails a multi-faceted approach, including building an emergency fund to cover unexpected expenses, obtaining appropriate insurance coverage for health, home, and life, and diversifying investments to mitigate risk. Additionally, practicing prudent budgeting and avoiding excessive debt can safeguard your financial stability. Staying vigilant against scams and fraud, monitoring your credit regularly, and maintaining a strong financial education are crucial in today's interconnected world. Ultimately, protecting your finances is about creating a robust financial foundation that can weather life's uncertainties and pave the way for a secure future.

A. Insurance Essentials

Insurance is a financial tool that provides protection against various risks and uncertainties that individuals and businesses face. From safeguarding health to protecting property and ensuring financial stability, different types of insurance play critical roles in managing risks. In this comprehensive exploration, we will delve into the various categories of insurance, shedding light on their purposes, mechanisms, and the importance they hold in the broader landscape of financial well-being.

Health Insurance

Health insurance is designed to cover medical expenses, offering financial protection in the event of illness, injury, or routine medical care. Health insurance plans can include coverage for doctor visits, hospital stays, prescription medications, and preventive care. These plans can be obtained through employers, government programs like Medicare or Medicaid, or individual policies. The aim is to mitigate the financial burden of healthcare costs, ensuring that individuals can access necessary medical services without incurring exorbitant expenses.

Auto Insurance

Auto insurance is a legal requirement for vehicle owners and is designed to provide financial protection in the event of an accident or damage to the insured vehicle. It typically includes liability coverage for bodily injury and property damage, as well as coverage for the insured's own vehicle (comprehensive and collision coverage). Auto insurance not only protects against financial losses but also ensures compliance with legal requirements, making it an essential component for anyone who owns or operates a vehicle.

Life Insurance

Life insurance provides a financial safety net for loved ones in the event of the policyholder's death. There are various types of life insurance, including term life, whole life, and universal life. Term life insurance covers a specified period, paying out a death benefit if the insured passes away during that time. Whole life and universal life insurance provide coverage for the entire life of the policyholder and often include a cash value component that grows over time. Life insurance serves as a crucial component of financial planning, particularly for those with dependents, as it can replace lost income, cover debts, and facilitate a smooth financial transition for surviving family members.

Homeowners Insurance

Homeowners insurance is designed to protect homeowners from financial losses related to their property. It covers damage or loss to the home's structure and contents due to perils such as fire, theft, or natural disasters. Additionally, homeowners insurance typically includes liability coverage, protecting homeowners in the event that someone is injured on their property. For those who rent instead of own, renters insurance serves a similar purpose, protecting personal belongings and offering liability coverage within a rented dwelling.

Renters Insurance

Renters insurance is tailored for individuals who lease or rent their living spaces. While landlords generally have insurance to cover the structure of the building, renters insurance protects the tenant's personal property within the rented space. It also provides liability coverage, offering financial protection if the tenant is found responsible for damage to the property or if someone is injured while on the premises.

Disability Insurance

Disability insurance is designed to replace a portion of income if the policyholder becomes unable to work due to a disabling injury or illness. Short-term disability insurance covers a temporary inability to work, while long-term disability insurance provides coverage for extended periods, potentially until retirement. Disability insurance helps maintain financial stability by offering a source of income even when the policyholder is unable to earn a salary due to disability.

Umbrella Insurance

Umbrella insurance is a form of liability insurance that provides additional coverage beyond the limits of other insurance policies. It serves as a financial safety net, offering protection against lawsuits and claims that exceed the coverage limits of standard policies, such as auto or homeowners insurance. Umbrella insurance is particularly relevant for individuals with substantial assets, as it can shield them from the financial fallout of significant liability claims.

Travel Insurance

Travel insurance is designed to cover unexpected events that may occur during a trip. This can include trip cancellations, interruptions, or delays, as well as coverage for medical emergencies while traveling. Travel insurance provides peace of mind, ensuring that financial losses related to travel disruptions or unforeseen circumstances are mitigated.

Pet Insurance

Pet insurance covers veterinary expenses for the treatment of illnesses or injuries in pets. It helps pet owners manage the cost of veterinary care, making it more affordable to provide necessary medical attention for their furry companions. Pet insurance typically covers a range of veterinary services, including surgeries, medications, and preventive care.

Business Insurance

Business insurance encompasses various types of coverage to protect businesses from financial losses. This can include property insurance to cover damage to business premises, liability insurance to protect against legal claims, and business interruption insurance to provide financial support if operations are disrupted. Specific types of business insurance, such as professional liability insurance or product liability insurance, cater to the unique risks associated with specific industries.

Cyber Insurance

In the digital age, cyber insurance has become increasingly relevant. It covers financial losses resulting from cyberattacks, data breaches, and other cyber threats. Cyber insurance helps businesses mitigate the financial impact of cyber incidents, including the costs of data recovery, legal expenses, and notification to affected parties.

Long-Term Care Insurance

Long-term care insurance provides coverage for the costs associated with long-term care services, including nursing home care, assisted living, and in-home care. It helps individuals plan for the potential expenses of extended healthcare services in later life, ensuring that they have financial support for necessary care without depleting personal assets.

Conclusion

Understanding the diverse landscape of insurance is essential for creating a comprehensive risk management strategy. Each type of insurance serves a unique purpose, offering financial protection against specific risks and uncertainties. By carefully selecting and customizing insurance coverage based on individual needs, individuals and businesses can navigate life's uncertainties with greater confidence and financial security. Ultimately, insurance is a critical tool for managing risk and protecting the hard-earned assets and well-being of individuals and their loved ones.

B. Estate Planning

Estate planning is a comprehensive process that involves
making crucial decisions about the distribution of your assets,
managing your affairs during incapacity, and ensuring that your
wishes are carried out after your passing. This multifaceted
endeavor aims to protect your financial legacy, minimize taxes,
and provide for your loved ones according to your intentions.
In this in-depth exploration of estate planning, we will delve
into two central components: Wills and Trusts, and Inheritance
and Legacy Planning.

1. Wills and Trusts

Wills

A will is a legal document that outlines your wishes for the
distribution of your assets and the guardianship of minor
children (if applicable) after your death. It serves as a
foundational component of estate planning, providing clarity
and legal authority over the disposition of your estate.

Key Aspects of Wills

- **Asset Distribution:** Wills specify how your assets,
  including real estate, investments, personal property,
  and valuables, should be distributed among
  beneficiaries, which can include family members,
  friends, and charitable organizations.

- **Executor:** A will designates an executor, a trusted individual or entity responsible for managing the probate process and ensuring your wishes are carried out. It is essential to select an executor who is organized, financially savvy, and capable of handling administrative responsibilities.

- **Guardianship:** If you have minor children, a will allows you to nominate a guardian who will assume legal responsibility for their care in the event of your passing. This decision is crucial for ensuring the well-being of your children.

- **Debts and Taxes:** Wills can address outstanding debts and specify how they should be settled from your estate. However, it's important to note that a will alone does not necessarily shield your estate from estate taxes, which can be a substantial consideration for high-net-worth individuals.

Benefits of Wills

- **Control:** Wills grant you full control over the distribution of your assets, allowing you to specify precisely how your estate should be divided.

- **Clarity:** A well-drafted will provides clarity to your loved ones, reducing the likelihood of disputes and misunderstandings after your passing.

- **Legal Framework:** Wills create a legally recognized framework for your wishes, ensuring they are upheld according to the law.

Trusts

Trusts are versatile legal arrangements that can serve a multitude of purposes within estate planning. They enable you to transfer assets to a trustee who manages and distributes them according to your specified terms. Trusts offer greater flexibility, privacy, and often, tax advantages compared to wills.

Key Aspects of Trusts

- **Living Trusts:** Living trusts, also known as revocable trusts, are created during your lifetime and allow you to manage and retain control of your assets. You can modify or revoke the trust as long as you are mentally competent.

- **Irrevocable Trusts:** Irrevocable trusts, once established, cannot be altered or revoked without the consent of the beneficiaries. These trusts are often used for specific purposes, such as minimizing estate taxes or protecting assets from creditors.

- **Asset Protection Trusts:** Asset protection trusts shield assets from creditors, making them useful for individuals in high-liability professions or those seeking to safeguard their wealth.

- **Special Needs Trusts:** Special needs trusts provide for individuals with disabilities without jeopardizing their eligibility for government assistance programs.

- **Charitable Trusts:** Charitable trusts allow you to support charitable causes while potentially receiving tax benefits. Examples include charitable remainder trusts and charitable lead trusts.

Benefits of Trusts

- **Privacy:** Unlike wills, trusts are generally private documents, and their contents are not subject to public scrutiny through the probate process.

- **Avoidance of Probate:** Assets placed in trusts often bypass the probate process, facilitating faster asset distribution and potentially reducing associated costs.

- **Tax Efficiency:** Certain trusts can offer tax benefits, including estate tax reduction or avoidance, making them valuable tools for wealth preservation.

2. Inheritance and Legacy Planning

Inheritance and legacy planning encompass a broader perspective on wealth transfer and the lasting impact of your financial legacy. While wills and trusts play central roles in asset distribution, inheritance and legacy planning delve into the following considerations:

Family Dynamics

Understanding family dynamics and relationships is crucial for effective inheritance and legacy planning. Open communication among family members about your wishes, values, and intentions can help prevent conflicts and misunderstandings down the line. It's essential to consider how inheritances may impact beneficiaries, both individually and in terms of family dynamics.

Financial Education

Inheritance and legacy planning can involve educating heirs about financial matters, wealth management, and responsible stewardship of assets. Providing financial literacy and guidance can empower beneficiaries to make informed decisions and ensure the continued growth and preservation of family wealth.

Philanthropy and Giving

Many individuals incorporate charitable giving and philanthropy into their legacy planning. Establishing family foundations, endowments, or charitable trusts allows you to support causes that matter to you while leaving a lasting impact on your community or the world.

Tax Planning

Inheritance and legacy planning often involve strategic tax planning to minimize estate taxes and maximize the amount passed on to beneficiaries. This can include gifting strategies, utilizing the annual gift tax exclusion, and optimizing the use of trusts.

Succession Planning for Businesses

For business owners, succession planning is a critical aspect of inheritance and legacy planning. Determining who will take over the business and ensuring a smooth transition is essential for preserving its value and maintaining its legacy.

Multigenerational Planning

Legacy planning often extends beyond immediate beneficiaries to multiple generations. Establishing structures like family trusts or holding companies can help manage and distribute wealth over the long term while preserving family values and traditions.

Professional Guidance

Inheritance and legacy planning can be complex, requiring expertise in legal, financial, and tax matters. Engaging estate planning attorneys, financial advisors, and tax professionals can help ensure that your plans are well-structured and legally sound.

Review and Adaptation

Legacy plans should be regularly reviewed and adapted to reflect changes in your financial situation, family dynamics, and legislative developments. Flexibility in planning allows you to respond to evolving circumstances effectively.

Conclusion

Estate planning is a comprehensive and dynamic process that involves much more than drafting wills and establishing trusts. It encompasses a holistic approach to safeguarding your legacy, ensuring the well-being of loved ones, and leaving a lasting impact on the world. By carefully considering family dynamics, financial education, philanthropy, tax planning, and succession, you can create a legacy plan that aligns with your values and provides a solid foundation for generations to come. Proper estate planning offers the peace of mind that comes from knowing your wishes will be honored and your financial legacy will endure.

VI. Financial Milestones

Financial milestones are significant achievements in one's financial journey that mark progress towards long-term goals and financial security. These milestones can include paying off high-interest debts, building an emergency fund, achieving a specific level of retirement savings, buying a home, or funding a child's education. Each milestone represents a step toward greater financial independence, stability, and freedom. Setting, tracking, and celebrating these milestones can provide motivation and a sense of accomplishment on the path to financial success. They serve as guideposts, helping individuals and families navigate their financial journey and make informed decisions about their future.

A. Buying a Home

Buying a home is a significant financial milestone and a major life decision. It represents not only a place of shelter but also a long-term investment. The process typically involves saving for a down payment, securing a mortgage, and carefully selecting a property that suits both current needs and future plans. Homeownership can offer stability, build equity over time, and provide a sense of pride and ownership. However, it also comes with responsibilities like property maintenance, insurance, and property taxes. Careful consideration of one's financial situation and long-term goals is essential when embarking on the journey to buy a home, as it can have a profound impact on overall financial well-being.

1. Mortgage Options

Purchasing a home is a significant financial milestone, and for most people, it involves securing a mortgage to make this dream a reality. Mortgages are complex financial instruments, and various options exist to suit different needs and financial situations. In this comprehensive guide, we will delve into the world of mortgage options, helping you understand the types of mortgages available, their advantages, and considerations.

Fixed-Rate Mortgages

Advantages: Fixed-rate mortgages offer stability and predictability. Your interest rate remains constant throughout the life of the loan, allowing for consistent monthly payments. This predictability makes it easier to budget and plan for the long term.

Considerations: Fixed-rate mortgages may have slightly higher initial interest rates compared to adjustable-rate mortgages (ARMs). However, they can be a wise choice if you plan to stay in your home for an extended period or prefer the security of knowing your monthly payments won't change.

Adjustable-Rate Mortgages (ARMs)

Advantages: ARMs typically start with lower initial interest rates, making them more affordable in the short term. They often have rate adjustment caps, which limit how much the interest rate can increase during each adjustment period.

Considerations: ARMs can become riskier over time if interest rates rise significantly. Borrowers need to carefully consider their financial situation and ability to handle potential payment increases in the future. ARMs may be suitable for those who plan to sell or refinance the home before the initial fixed-rate period ends.

FHA Loans

Advantages: Federal Housing Administration (FHA) loans are government-insured mortgages that allow for lower down payments (typically as low as 3.5%) and more flexible credit requirements, making homeownership more accessible for first-time buyers and those with limited credit histories.

Considerations: FHA loans require mortgage insurance premiums, which can increase the overall cost of the loan. Borrowers must also adhere to specific property standards, and loan limits may apply based on location.

VA Loans

Advantages: Veterans Affairs (VA) loans are available to eligible veterans, service members, and their families. These loans typically offer 100% financing (no down payment required), competitive interest rates, and lenient credit requirements.

Considerations: VA loans may involve a one-time funding fee, and borrowers must meet specific eligibility criteria. However, they can be an excellent option for those who have served in the military and meet the qualifications.

USDA Loans

Advantages: United States Department of Agriculture (USDA) loans are designed for eligible rural and suburban homebuyers. They offer 100% financing, competitive interest rates, and low mortgage insurance rates.

Considerations: USDA loans are location-dependent and subject to income limits. Borrowers must purchase homes in USDA-eligible areas and meet income requirements based on family size.

Jumbo Loans

Advantages: Jumbo loans are used for high-value properties that exceed the conforming loan limits set by Fannie Mae and Freddie Mac. They allow buyers to finance more expensive homes while still benefiting from competitive interest rates.

Considerations: Jumbo loans typically require larger down payments and may have stricter credit requirements. Interest rates can also be slightly higher than those for conforming loans.

Interest-Only Mortgages

Advantages: Interest-only mortgages allow borrowers to make lower monthly payments for a specified initial period by paying only the interest on the loan. This option can free up cash flow for other investments or financial goals.

Considerations: After the initial interest-only period, borrowers must begin paying principal and interest, which can result in significantly higher monthly payments. Interest-only mortgages carry more risk and may not be suitable for everyone.

Balloon Mortgages

Advantages: Balloon mortgages offer low monthly payments for a specific period, similar to interest-only loans. However, at the end of the term, borrowers must pay off the remaining loan balance in a lump sum or refinance the loan.

Considerations: Balloon mortgages can be risky, as borrowers must be prepared to handle the substantial balloon payment when it comes due. They are not recommended for those who are uncertain about their ability to refinance or pay off the remaining balance.

Conclusion

Selecting the right mortgage option is a critical decision in the homebuying process, one that should align with your financial goals and long-term plans. It's essential to evaluate your financial situation, consider factors like the length of time you plan to stay in the home, and compare interest rates and terms from various lenders. Consulting with a qualified mortgage professional can provide valuable guidance and help you make an informed decision that sets you on the path to homeownership and financial stability.

2. Homeownership Costs

Homeownership is a significant milestone that brings numerous benefits, including stability, pride of ownership, and the potential for long-term wealth building. However, it also entails a range of costs and financial responsibilities that extend well beyond the purchase price of the home. In this comprehensive guide, we will explore the various expenses associated with homeownership to help you make informed financial decisions and manage your budget effectively.

Mortgage Payments

The most substantial homeownership cost for many is the monthly mortgage payment. This payment consists of two main components: principal and interest. The principal portion goes towards paying down the loan balance, while the interest represents the cost of borrowing the money. Depending on your mortgage type and terms, your monthly payment can remain fixed (with a fixed-rate mortgage) or fluctuate (with an adjustable-rate mortgage).

Property Taxes

Property taxes are assessed by local governments and are based on the assessed value of your home. The tax revenue supports various community services, such as schools, infrastructure, and public safety. Property tax rates can vary widely by location, so it's crucial to research the rates in your area and budget for these ongoing expenses.

Homeowners Insurance

Homeowners insurance provides essential protection for your property against unexpected events, such as fire, theft, or natural disasters. The cost of insurance premiums can vary based on factors like the home's location, its age and condition, and the coverage options you choose. Lenders typically require homeowners insurance as part of the mortgage agreement.

Private Mortgage Insurance (PMI)

If you make a down payment of less than 20% of the home's purchase price, your lender may require you to pay for private mortgage insurance. PMI protects the lender in case of default. The cost of PMI is added to your monthly mortgage payment and can be a significant expense until you've built up sufficient equity in the home.

Home Maintenance and Repairs

Owning a home means taking on the responsibility of maintenance and repairs. This includes routine tasks like landscaping, cleaning, and HVAC system maintenance, as well as unexpected repairs, such as a leaky roof or a malfunctioning appliance. Budgeting for these expenses is essential to keep your home in good condition and prevent larger, costlier issues down the line.

Homeowners Association (HOA) Fees

If your property is part of a homeowners association, you may be required to pay monthly or annual HOA fees. These fees cover the cost of maintaining common areas, amenities, and community services. It's important to understand the HOA rules and fee structure before purchasing a property in an HOA-managed community.

Utilities

Utilities such as electricity, water, gas, and sewage are ongoing expenses associated with homeownership. The cost of utilities can vary depending on factors like your location, the size of your home, and your usage patterns. Energy-efficient upgrades and practices can help reduce utility costs over time.

Home Renovations and Upgrades

Many homeowners choose to make improvements to their homes over time, whether for aesthetic reasons or to enhance functionality. Renovations and upgrades can be significant expenses, and it's essential to budget for them based on your priorities and long-term plans.

Closing Costs

When you purchase a home, you'll incur closing costs, which include various fees and charges related to the transaction. These costs typically include fees for the appraisal, home inspection, title search, loan origination, and more. It's important to budget for these expenses in addition to your down payment.

Moving Expenses

The cost of moving to your new home can also be significant. This includes expenses such as hiring a moving company, renting a truck, or purchasing packing supplies. Planning and budgeting for these costs can help ensure a smooth transition to your new home.

Conclusion

While homeownership brings numerous benefits, it also comes with a range of financial responsibilities and costs that extend well beyond the initial purchase price. To successfully navigate the financial aspects of homeownership, it's crucial to create a comprehensive budget that includes mortgage payments, property taxes, insurance, maintenance, and other ongoing expenses. Being financially prepared for homeownership ensures that you can enjoy the advantages of owning a home while maintaining your overall financial stability and security.

B. Marriage and Family

Marriage and starting a family are significant life events that bring about a host of financial milestones and responsibilities. These milestones often include combining finances, setting joint financial goals, and preparing for your children's education. In this comprehensive guide, we will explore the financial aspects of marriage and family life, helping you navigate these transitions with confidence and strategic planning.

1. Combining Finances

Joint Accounts vs. Separate Accounts

One of the first financial decisions married couples face is whether to maintain separate accounts, open joint accounts, or use a combination of both. Each approach has its advantages and considerations. Joint accounts can simplify bill payments and joint financial goals, while separate accounts offer independence and can be useful for managing individual expenses or discretionary spending.

Budgeting and Financial Goals

Creating a joint budget is crucial for managing household expenses and savings. Discuss your financial goals as a couple, such as buying a home, saving for retirement, or funding your children's education. A well-structured budget can help you allocate funds to achieve these objectives.

Emergency Fund

Establishing an emergency fund is essential for both married couples and families. This fund should cover at least three to six months' worth of living expenses and serve as a financial safety net in case of unexpected events like medical emergencies or job loss.

Insurance and Estate Planning

Review and update your insurance policies, including health, life, and disability insurance, to ensure adequate coverage for both spouses and any dependents. Additionally, consider creating or updating your estate plan, which may include wills, trusts, and powers of attorney to protect your assets and provide for your loved ones in case of incapacity or death.

2. Saving for Children's Education

529 College Savings Plans

A 529 college savings plan is a tax-advantaged account designed specifically for educational expenses. Contributions to these plans can grow tax-free, and withdrawals for qualified education expenses are also tax-free. Opening a 529 plan early and regularly contributing to it can help build a substantial fund for your children's higher education.

Custodial Accounts

Custodial accounts, often known as Uniform Gifts to Minors Act (UGMA) or Uniform Transfers to Minors Act (UTMA) accounts, allow parents to invest on behalf of their children. While these accounts lack some of the tax advantages of 529 plans, they offer more flexibility in how the funds can be used.

Scholarships and Financial Aid

Encourage your children to seek scholarships and financial aid opportunities. Completing the Free Application for Federal Student Aid (FAFSA) can help determine eligibility for federal grants, loans, and work-study programs. Additionally, researching and applying for scholarships can significantly reduce the financial burden of higher education.

Education Savings Timeline

Start saving for your children's education as early as possible to maximize the growth potential of your investments. A longer time horizon allows you to benefit from compound interest and potentially accumulate more funds for educational expenses.

Balancing Retirement and Education Savings

It's essential to strike a balance between saving for your children's education and your retirement. While you may want to prioritize your children's future, it's crucial to ensure your own financial security in retirement. Evaluate your financial situation and seek professional guidance if needed to strike the right balance.

Conclusion

Marriage and starting a family are transformative life events that bring both joy and financial responsibilities. Combining finances, setting financial goals, and preparing for your children's education require open communication, careful planning, and a shared commitment to financial responsibility. By addressing these milestones proactively and aligning your financial strategies with your family's long-term objectives, you can create a solid foundation for a financially secure and fulfilling married life and family journey.

C. Retirement and Financial Independence

Retirement and financial independence represent the culmination of a lifetime of diligent financial planning and disciplined saving. Retirement signifies the point at which individuals choose to step away from traditional employment to enjoy the fruits of their labor and pursue personal passions. Achieving financial independence means having the financial resources and security to support one's desired lifestyle without the need for active employment income. This milestone often involves building a substantial retirement nest egg, reducing debt, and establishing passive income streams. Both retirement and financial independence reflect the realization of long-held dreams and the freedom to live life on one's own terms, unburdened by financial constraints. It underscores the importance of sound financial planning and prudent investment strategies throughout one's working years.

1. Retirement Accounts and Strategies

Retirement planning is a critical aspect of financial well-being, and retirement accounts play a central role in helping individuals secure their financial futures. These accounts offer tax advantages, long-term growth potential, and a structured way to save for retirement. In this comprehensive guide, we will explore various types of retirement accounts and strategies to help you make informed decisions and work toward a comfortable retirement.

Types of Retirement Accounts

401(k) Plans

401(k) plans are employer-sponsored retirement accounts that allow employees to contribute a portion of their pre-tax income into an investment account. Employers may offer matching contributions up to a certain percentage, effectively doubling the employee's savings. 401(k)s offer tax-deferred growth, meaning you don't pay taxes on contributions or earnings until you withdraw the funds in retirement. These plans are subject to annual contribution limits set by the IRS.

Individual Retirement Accounts (IRAs)

IRAs are individual retirement accounts that offer tax advantages for retirement savings. There are two primary types of IRAs:

Traditional IRA: Contributions to a traditional IRA may be tax-deductible, reducing your current taxable income. Earnings in the account grow tax-deferred until withdrawal in retirement.

Roth IRA: Roth IRAs, on the other hand, do not provide immediate tax deductions for contributions. However, qualified withdrawals in retirement are entirely tax-free, making Roth IRAs an attractive option for tax-free income in retirement.

Both types of IRAs have annual contribution limits, and eligibility may depend on factors such as income and employment status.

403(b) Plans

403(b) plans are similar to 401(k) plans but are typically offered by nonprofit organizations, schools, and certain government entities. They allow employees to make pre-tax contributions for retirement and often feature employer contributions or matches. Contributions to a 403(b) plan grow tax-deferred until distribution.

Simplified Employee Pension (SEP) IRAs

SEP IRAs are designed for self-employed individuals and small business owners. These plans allow for tax-deductible contributions, and the business can contribute on behalf of eligible employees. SEP IRAs offer flexibility and higher contribution limits compared to traditional and Roth IRAs.

Retirement Savings Strategies

1. **Start Early:** One of the most effective retirement strategies is to begin saving as early as possible. The power of compound interest means that even modest contributions can grow significantly over time. Starting early gives your investments more time to compound and grow.
2. **Maximize Employer Matches:** If your employer offers a retirement plan with a matching contribution, take full advantage of it. Matching contributions effectively double your savings, providing an immediate boost to your retirement nest egg.

3. **Diversify Your Investments:** Diversification is a key strategy for managing risk in your retirement portfolio. Spread your investments across different asset classes, such as stocks, bonds, and real estate, to reduce exposure to the volatility of any one market.

4. **Increase Contributions Over Time:** As your income grows or expenses decrease, consider increasing your retirement contributions. Many retirement plans allow for automatic contribution increases, making it easier to save more as you earn more.

5. **Take Advantage of Catch-Up Contributions:** For those age 50 and older, retirement account rules allow for catch-up contributions, which are higher annual contribution limits. These catch-up contributions can help boost your retirement savings in the years leading up to retirement.

6. **Review and Rebalance Your Portfolio:** Regularly review your retirement portfolio to ensure it aligns with your risk tolerance and long-term goals. Rebalancing may be necessary to maintain your desired asset allocation.

7. **Consider Professional Advice:** Seeking advice from a financial advisor or retirement planner can be invaluable in creating a personalized retirement strategy. They can help you assess your financial situation, set realistic goals, and develop a tailored investment plan.

2. Achieving Financial Freedom

Retirement accounts and strategies are essential tools for building financial security in retirement. Whether through employer-sponsored plans like 401(k)s, individual retirement accounts (IRAs), or other retirement vehicles, taking advantage of these tax-advantaged savings options can significantly impact your retirement readiness. By starting early, contributing consistently, and diversifying your investments, you can work toward a comfortable retirement that aligns with your financial goals and aspirations. Regularly reviewing and adjusting your retirement strategy ensures that you stay on track to achieve your retirement dreams.

Achieving financial freedom is the ultimate goal for many individuals, representing a state of financial security and independence where you have the freedom to make choices based on your desires and values rather than financial constraints. It involves careful planning, disciplined saving, and smart investment decisions over time. Financial freedom means having sufficient assets and passive income streams to cover your living expenses and pursue your life goals, whether that means retiring early, starting your own business, traveling the world, or supporting charitable causes. It's a journey that requires commitment, financial literacy, and the ability to make wise financial choices, ultimately leading to a life where you have the power to control your financial destiny and live life on your own terms.

VII. Navigating Financial Challenges

In life, financial challenges are an inevitable part of the journey. From economic downturns and job loss to unexpected expenses and the toll of financial stress on mental health, these challenges can test one's resilience and financial stability. However, with the right strategies and mindset, individuals can not only weather these storms but also emerge stronger and more financially secure. In this comprehensive guide, we will explore various financial challenges and provide actionable advice on how to navigate them effectively.

A. Economic Downturns and Job Loss

Economic Downturns

Economic downturns, such as recessions or financial crises, can have far-reaching effects on individuals and families. Jobs may become scarce, investments may decline in value, and overall economic uncertainty can create anxiety. Here are some strategies for navigating economic downturns:

- **Emergency Fund:** Maintaining an emergency fund with three to six months' worth of living expenses can provide a financial safety net during periods of job loss or economic uncertainty. This fund can cover essential expenses and ease financial stress.

- **Budgeting:** Creating a budget and tracking expenses can help identify areas where you can cut back during tough times. This can extend the longevity of your emergency fund and keep your finances in check.

- **Diversified Investments:** Diversifying your investment portfolio can help reduce the impact of market downturns. A mix of stocks, bonds, and other assets can provide stability and potential for growth.

- **Seeking New Opportunities:** In challenging job markets, it may be necessary to explore new career opportunities or develop additional skills to enhance employability.

Job Loss

Job loss is a daunting financial challenge that can impact both income and mental well-being. However, there are steps individuals can take to mitigate its effects:

- **Unemployment Benefits:** If eligible, apply for unemployment benefits promptly. These benefits can provide temporary financial support while you search for new employment.

- **Networking:** Leverage your professional network to uncover job opportunities. Networking can often be more effective than online job searches.

- **Temporary Work:** Consider taking on temporary or part-time work to maintain income while searching for a long-term position.

- **Update Your Skills:** Use the period of unemployment to enhance your skills through training, certification programs, or education, which can make you more competitive in the job market.

B. Dealing with Unexpected Expenses

Unexpected expenses, whether medical bills, car repairs, or home emergencies, can disrupt your financial stability. Planning for such contingencies is crucial:

- **Emergency Fund:** We cannot overemphasize the importance of an emergency fund. This fund should cover not only job loss but also unexpected expenses. Having liquid savings ensures you won't have to rely on high-interest credit or loans.
- **Insurance:** Appropriate insurance coverage, including health, auto, and homeowners or renters insurance, can protect you from significant financial burdens in the face of unexpected events.
- **Prioritize Savings:** Regularly contribute to savings accounts designated for specific purposes, such as a car repair fund or a medical expenses fund. These

earmarked savings can provide peace of mind when these expenses arise.

- **Budget Flexibility:** Create a flexible budget that allows you to adapt to unexpected expenses without major disruptions. Allocating a portion of your income to a "miscellaneous" or "contingency" category can provide flexibility.

C. Handling Financial Stress and Mental Health

Financial stress can take a toll on mental health and overall well-being. It's essential to recognize the signs of financial stress and implement strategies to mitigate its effects:

- **Seek Support:** Reach out to friends, family, or support groups to discuss your financial concerns. Talking about your challenges can provide emotional relief and lead to helpful advice.
- **Professional Help:** If financial stress becomes overwhelming and affects your mental health, consider seeking assistance from a therapist or counselor. They can help you manage stress and develop coping strategies.
- **Mindfulness and Stress Reduction:** Practice mindfulness and stress-reduction techniques, such as meditation, deep breathing exercises, or yoga. These practices can help reduce anxiety associated with financial worries.

- **Financial Education:** Increase your financial literacy and knowledge. Understanding your financial situation and having a plan can alleviate anxiety and improve decision-making.
- **Set Realistic Goals:** Setting achievable financial goals can provide a sense of purpose and direction. These goals can be short-term, like paying off credit card debt, or long-term, such as saving for retirement.
- **Budget and Track Expenses:** A well-structured budget can offer financial control and peace of mind. Tracking expenses helps identify areas where you can cut back and allocate funds to essential priorities.

Conclusion

Financial challenges are a part of life, but with the right strategies and mindset, individuals can navigate them effectively. Establishing financial safety nets like emergency funds, maintaining diversified investments, and seeking professional advice when needed can provide stability during economic downturns and job loss. Planning for unexpected expenses through savings and insurance can minimize their impact. Finally, addressing financial stress through support networks, mindfulness, and financial education can lead to better mental health and overall well-being. By proactively tackling these challenges, individuals can build financial resilience and achieve a more secure and stress-free financial future.

VIII. Advanced Financial Strategies

A. Investment Diversification

Diversifying your investment portfolio is a fundamental strategy for managing risk and achieving long-term financial success. However, as your financial knowledge and wealth grow, you may consider advanced diversification strategies to further optimize your investments. In this guide, we will explore some advanced financial strategies for investment diversification to help you build a more robust and resilient portfolio.

1. Asset Class Diversification

While basic diversification involves spreading investments across different asset classes, advanced diversification drills down further. Beyond stocks and bonds, consider diversifying within asset classes. For instance:

- **Equity Diversification:** Within the stock portion of your portfolio, allocate investments across various sectors (e.g., technology, healthcare, consumer goods) and geographic regions (e.g., domestic and international markets). This reduces your exposure to the performance of a single sector or region.

- **Bond Diversification:** In the fixed-income portion of your portfolio, diversify among different types of bonds, including government, corporate, municipal, and international bonds. Varying maturities can also help manage interest rate risk.

2. Alternative Investments:

Alternative investments, such as real estate, private equity, hedge funds, and commodities, can provide diversification beyond traditional asset classes. These assets often have low correlations with stocks and bonds, which means their performance may not move in lockstep with the broader market. Incorporating alternative investments into your portfolio can enhance diversification and potentially reduce risk.

3. Factor-Based Investing:

Factor-based investing involves targeting specific factors or characteristics associated with higher returns. Some common factors include:

- **Value:** Investing in undervalued stocks with low price-to-earnings ratios.

- **Momentum:** Allocating to assets that have exhibited recent positive price momentum.

- **Quality:** Selecting investments with strong fundamentals, such as low debt levels and high profitability.

- **Size:** Favoring small-cap stocks, which historically have shown higher returns over time.

Factor-based investing can be achieved through factor-specific exchange-traded funds (ETFs) or mutual funds, allowing you to fine-tune your portfolio based on your risk tolerance and investment objectives.

4. Tactical Asset Allocation:

Tactical asset allocation involves actively adjusting your portfolio's asset allocation in response to changing market conditions. This strategy allows you to capitalize on short-term opportunities and mitigate risks. For example, during periods of market volatility, you might reduce equity exposure and increase allocations to safer assets like bonds or cash. Tactical asset allocation requires a deep understanding of financial markets and economic indicators.

5. Tax-Efficient Investing:

Tax-efficient investing involves optimizing your investment decisions to minimize taxes. Strategies may include tax-loss harvesting, where you sell losing investments to offset gains, and using tax-advantaged accounts like IRAs and 401(k)s to shield your investments from taxes. Efficiently managing taxes can significantly impact your overall returns.

6. Portfolio Rebalancing:

Regularly rebalancing your portfolio ensures that your asset allocation remains in line with your investment goals and risk tolerance. When certain assets outperform others, your portfolio's allocation can become skewed. Rebalancing involves selling some of the outperforming assets and buying underperforming ones to restore the desired balance. This process helps you sell high and buy low, a fundamental principle of investing.

7. Risk Parity Strategy:

A risk parity strategy aims to achieve balanced risk across different asset classes rather than balanced capital allocation. It involves allocating more capital to asset classes with lower historical volatility and less to those with higher volatility. Risk parity strategies seek to achieve consistent returns while managing risk.

8. Multi-Asset Investing:

Multi-asset investing involves combining various asset classes, factors, and strategies into a single investment vehicle. These diversified funds are managed by professionals who allocate assets based on market conditions and objectives. Multi-asset funds can simplify complex diversification strategies for individual investors.

Conclusion

As you progress in your financial journey, advanced diversification strategies can help you build a more resilient and efficient investment portfolio. These strategies go beyond basic asset allocation to fine-tune your investments, manage risk, and optimize returns. Remember that advanced strategies may involve higher complexity and may not be suitable for all investors. Consulting with a financial advisor or investment professional can help you navigate the intricacies of advanced diversification and tailor them to your unique financial goals and risk tolerance.

B. Tax Optimization

Tax optimization is a critical aspect of managing your finances, and advanced strategies can help you minimize your tax liability while maximizing your wealth. These strategies go beyond the basics of tax planning and require careful consideration of your financial situation, goals, and the ever-changing tax landscape. In this guide, we'll explore advanced financial strategies for tax optimization that can help you keep more of your hard-earned money.

1. Tax-Efficient Investment Portfolio:

Building a tax-efficient investment portfolio involves selecting investments and strategies that minimize taxable events. Some key tactics include:

- **Tax-Efficient Fund Selection:** Invest in tax-efficient mutual funds or exchange-traded funds (ETFs) that generate fewer taxable distributions. These funds are designed to minimize capital gains and income distributions.

- **Tax-Loss Harvesting:** Implement a tax-loss harvesting strategy by selling investments that have declined in value to offset capital gains in your portfolio. Be mindful of wash-sale rules that may apply.

- **Asset Location:** Allocate assets strategically among taxable and tax-advantaged accounts. For example, place tax-efficient investments like index funds in taxable accounts and less tax-efficient investments like bonds in tax-advantaged accounts.

- **Qualified Dividend and Long-Term Capital Gains Tax Rates:** Take advantage of lower tax rates on qualified dividends and long-term capital gains, which are generally more favorable than ordinary income tax rates. This may involve holding investments for more extended periods.

2. **Retirement Account Maximization:**

Retirement accounts like 401(k)s, IRAs, and Roth IRAs offer valuable tax benefits that can be optimized for long-term wealth growth:

- **Roth IRA Conversion:** Consider converting traditional IRA funds to a Roth IRA, paying taxes on the converted amount at your current tax rate. Roth IRAs offer tax-free withdrawals in retirement, which can be advantageous for future tax planning.

- **Backdoor Roth IRA:** If your income exceeds the eligibility limits for a Roth IRA, explore the backdoor Roth IRA strategy. This involves making nondeductible contributions to a traditional IRA and then converting it to a Roth IRA.

- **Qualified Charitable Distributions (QCDs):** If you're over 70½ and have required minimum distributions (RMDs) from retirement accounts, consider making QCDs to charitable organizations. These distributions count toward your RMDs and are excluded from your taxable income.

3. Estate Planning and Wealth Transfer:

Advanced tax optimization strategies extend to estate planning, ensuring the efficient transfer of wealth to heirs:

- **Gift Tax Exclusion:** Leverage the annual gift tax exclusion to gift assets to family members or beneficiaries without incurring gift taxes. For 2023, the exclusion is $16,000 per recipient.

- **Irrevocable Life Insurance Trust (ILIT):** Set up an ILIT to hold life insurance policies outside of your estate, potentially reducing estate tax liabilities.
- **Grantor Retained Annuity Trust (GRAT) and Qualified Personal Residence Trust (QPRT):** Explore GRATs and QPRTs to transfer assets or your primary residence to beneficiaries while minimizing gift and estate taxes.
- **Generation-Skipping Transfer (GST) Tax Planning:** For large estates, utilize GST planning to transfer wealth to grandchildren or subsequent generations, skipping a generation and reducing estate taxes.

4. Business Tax Strategies:

If you're a business owner or entrepreneur, there are advanced tax optimization strategies available:

- **Qualified Small Business Stock (QSBS):** Invest in QSBS to potentially benefit from a significant exclusion of capital gains upon sale, provided certain conditions are met.

- **Tax-Efficient Compensation:** Structuring your compensation package with tax-efficient elements like stock options, restricted stock units (RSUs), and deferred compensation can reduce your current tax liability.

- **Business Entity Optimization:** Choose the right business structure, such as an S Corporation or Limited Liability Company (LLC), to optimize tax treatment and liability protection.

C. Charitable and Philanthropic Giving

Advanced tax optimization strategies for charitable giving include:

- **Donor-Advised Funds (DAFs):** Contribute to a DAF to receive an immediate tax deduction while retaining control over when and how donations are distributed to charitable causes.

- **Charitable Remainder Trust (CRT):** Establish a CRT to receive income from donated assets for a specified period while benefiting a charitable organization, potentially reducing capital gains taxes.

- **Charitable Lead Trust (CLT):** A CLT can provide income to a charity for a defined period, after which the remaining assets pass to your heirs with potential estate tax benefits.

Conclusion

Advanced tax optimization strategies require a comprehensive and tailored approach to your financial situation and goals. They often involve complex rules and regulations, so consulting with a qualified tax professional or financial advisor is essential. By leveraging these advanced strategies, you can not only minimize your current tax liability but also create a tax-efficient financial plan that maximizes your long-term wealth and financial security.

IX. Staying Informed and Adapting

In an ever-changing financial landscape, staying informed and adapting to new circumstances are essential components of achieving and maintaining financial success. From keeping up with financial news to adjusting to life changes and revisiting financial goals, these practices ensure that your financial plan remains relevant, resilient, and aligned with your aspirations.

A. Keeping Up with Financial News

Staying informed about current financial news and market trends is fundamental for making informed financial decisions. Here's why it matters:

- **Market Insights:** Financial news provides insights into the performance of various asset classes, economic indicators, and market trends. This information can inform your investment strategy and help you identify opportunities and potential risks.
- **Interest Rates and Inflation:** Changes in interest rates and inflation rates can impact your savings, investments, and borrowing costs. Regularly monitoring these rates allows you to make adjustments to your financial plan as needed.
- **Economic Indicators:** Economic indicators such as GDP growth, unemployment rates, and consumer sentiment can influence your financial decisions.

Understanding these indicators helps you anticipate economic shifts and their potential effects on your finances.

- **Legislative Changes:** Tax laws, retirement regulations, and other financial regulations can change over time. Keeping up with these changes ensures that you can take advantage of tax-saving opportunities and comply with new rules.

To stay informed, consider subscribing to reputable financial news sources, following financial experts on social media, and attending webinars or seminars on relevant financial topics. The knowledge you gain will empower you to make more informed decisions.

B. Adapting to Life Changes

Life is filled with unexpected twists and turns, and adapting to these changes is crucial for financial success:

- **Career Transitions:** Job changes, promotions, or career shifts can impact your income, benefits, and retirement plans. Evaluate how these changes affect your financial goals and make necessary adjustments.
- **Family Changes:** Marriage, divorce, or having children can significantly alter your financial responsibilities and goals. Review your budget, insurance coverage, and

estate plan to ensure they align with your new circumstances.

- **Health Events:** Unexpected medical expenses or changes in health can disrupt your financial stability. Having adequate health insurance and an emergency fund can provide financial security during these times.
- **Market Volatility:** Financial markets are subject to periods of volatility and uncertainty. Develop a resilient investment strategy that can weather market fluctuations without jeopardizing your long-term goals.
- **Housing and Relocation:** Buying a home, relocating, or downsizing can have financial implications. Consider how these decisions impact your housing costs, property taxes, and overall budget.

C. Revisiting and Adjusting Financial Goals

Financial goals should evolve with your changing circumstances and aspirations. Here's how to revisit and adjust your financial goals effectively:

- **Regular Assessments:** Schedule periodic financial check-ins to review your progress toward existing goals and set new ones. This helps ensure that your financial plan remains relevant and motivating.
- **Prioritization:** As your life changes, you may need to reprioritize your financial goals. Consider which goals

are most important at each stage of life and allocate resources accordingly.

- **Smart Goals:** Ensure that your financial goals are Specific, Measurable, Achievable, Relevant, and Time-bound (SMART). This clarity makes it easier to track progress and stay motivated.
- **Emergency Fund:** Maintain an adequate emergency fund to cover unexpected expenses and financial setbacks. This safety net allows you to stay on track with your goals even when facing unforeseen challenges.
- **Retirement Planning:** Adjust your retirement savings goals as needed to account for changes in income, expenses, and retirement age. Regularly review your retirement plan to ensure you are on track for a comfortable retirement.
- **Seek Professional Guidance:** Consider consulting with a financial advisor or planner who can help you reassess your financial goals and create a customized plan that adapts to your evolving circumstances.

In summary, staying informed about financial news, adapting to life changes, and revisiting and adjusting your financial goals are vital components of financial success. By embracing these practices, you can build a resilient financial plan that withstands challenges and aligns with your evolving aspirations, ultimately leading to greater financial security and well-being.

X. Conclusion

A. Recap of Key Takeaways

We've covered many aspects of personal finance and managing one's financial life. Here are the key takeaways from each section.

I. Introduction:

- Personal finance is crucial.

- Setting financial goals is essential.

- The book will provide an overview of its content.

II. Building a Strong Financial Foundation:

- Budgeting is fundamental, involving creating, tracking, and establishing emergency funds.

- Managing debt requires understanding types, reduction strategies, and monitoring credit scores.

III. Saving and Investing:

- Saving for short-term goals involves planning and using high-yield savings accounts.

- Investing for long-term wealth includes different investment types, risk assessment, and retirement planning.

IV. Income Generation:

- Maximize earnings through career development and side hustles.

- Understand taxation and employ tax-efficient strategies.

V. Protecting Your Finances:

- Essential insurance coverage is vital.

- Estate planning includes wills, trusts, inheritance, and legacy planning.

VI. Financial Milestones:

- Key milestones like buying a home, marriage, and retirement are addressed.

- Financial aspects of each milestone are discussed.

VII. Navigating Financial Challenges:

- Strategies for coping with economic downturns, unexpected expenses, and managing financial stress.

VIII. Advanced Financial Strategies:

- Explore investment diversification, tax optimization, and charitable giving.

IX. Staying Informed and Adapting:

- Staying updated with financial news, adapting to life changes, and adjusting financial goals as needed.

In summary, this book aims to equip readers with essential personal finance knowledge, from budgeting and investing to income generation, protection, and addressing various financial challenges. It emphasizes adaptability and staying informed to achieve financial success and wellness.

B. Encouragement for Financial Success

Embarking on the journey to financial success is a remarkable endeavor, one that promises a future of security, freedom, and fulfillment. Remember that every small step you take today brings you closer to your goals tomorrow. It's not about how fast you progress, but about the consistent effort you put in.

Financial success is not a destination; it's a lifelong pursuit. As you navigate through budgeting, investing, and making wise financial decisions, know that setbacks and challenges are a natural part of the process. They provide valuable opportunities for learning and growth. Embrace them as stepping stones, not stumbling blocks, and use them to refine your financial strategies.

Stay motivated and envision the life you aspire to lead. Whether it's achieving debt freedom, owning your dream home, or securing a comfortable retirement, your financial journey is uniquely yours. Keep your goals in sight, adapt as needed, and celebrate your milestones along the way. Remember, the path to financial success is filled with resilience, determination, and the knowledge that your efforts today will shape a brighter, more prosperous tomorrow. You've got this!

C. Final Thoughts on Achieving Financial Wellness

In the pursuit of financial wellness, the journey is as important as the destination. Financial wellness isn't just about accumulating wealth; it's about achieving a state of balance, peace, and confidence in your financial life. It's a holistic approach that considers not only your bank account but also your overall well-being.

To attain financial wellness, always prioritize financial education and continuous learning. The world of finance is dynamic, and staying informed empowers you to make informed decisions. Be adaptable and willing to adjust your financial plan as circumstances change, and life takes unexpected turns.

Moreover, remember that financial wellness is deeply interconnected with your physical and mental well-being. Strive for a harmonious balance between your financial goals and your health, relationships, and personal values. Nurture a healthy relationship with money, one that aligns with your life's purpose and values.

Ultimately, financial wellness is not an end goal but an ongoing journey. It's about building a life that's not solely defined by financial success but enriched by a sense of security, contentment, and the freedom to pursue your passions and dreams. Embrace this journey with determination, patience, and the knowledge that you're taking steps toward a brighter and more fulfilling future.

XI. Appendices

A. Glossary of Financial Terms

401(k): A tax-advantaged retirement savings account offered by employers.

403(b) Plans: Retirement plans similar to 401(k) plans but typically offered by nonprofit organizations, schools, and certain government entities.

529 College Savings Plan: A tax-advantaged savings plan designed to help individuals and families save for future education expenses.

Adjustable-Rate Mortgage (ARM): A mortgage with an interest rate that may change periodically, typically based on an underlying benchmark interest rate.

Alternative Investments: Non-traditional investments like real estate, private equity, and commodities that provide diversification beyond stocks and bonds.

Amortization: The gradual repayment of a debt over time through regular installments.

Annual Percentage Rate (APR): The annual cost of borrowing, including interest and fees, expressed as a percentage of the loan amount.

Annuities: Annuities are financial products that provide a series of payments in exchange for a lump sum or periodic contributions. Some types of annuities offer guaranteed income streams during retirement.

Asset Allocation: Asset allocation is the strategic distribution of investment capital across different asset classes, such as stocks, bonds, real estate, and cash equivalents, to achieve financial goals while managing risk.

Asset Management: The professional management of investments and assets on behalf of individuals or institutions.

Asset Protection Trusts: Trusts designed to shield assets from creditors.

Asset: Anything of value owned by an individual, including cash, investments, real estate, and personal property.

Auto Insurance: Insurance required for vehicles, providing financial protection in case of accidents or damage.

Auto Loans: Loans used to purchase vehicles, often with lower interest rates compared to consumer debt.

Avalanche Method: A debt reduction strategy that focuses on paying off debts with the highest interest rates first to minimize total interest paid over time.

Backdoor Roth IRA: A strategy to contribute to a Roth IRA for high-income individuals by making nondeductible contributions to a traditional IRA and then converting it.

Balloon Mortgage: A mortgage with lower initial payments but a large final payment, often requiring refinancing or a lump-sum payment at the end of the term.

Bankruptcy: A legal process that allows individuals or businesses to discharge or reorganize debts.

Bear Market: A market characterized by falling stock prices and pessimism among investors.

Beneficiary: An individual or entity designated to receive assets or benefits from a trust or insurance policy.

Blue Chip Stock: A stock from a well-established, reputable company known for stability and reliability.

Blue Sky Laws: State regulations governing the issuance and sale of securities to protect investors from fraud.

Bond: A debt security that represents a loan made to a corporation or government, typically with periodic interest payments.

Budget: A financial plan that outlines income, expenses, and savings goals, helping individuals manage their finances.

Bull Market: A market characterized by rising stock prices and optimism among investors.

Bullion: Precious metals, such as gold or silver, in the form of bars, coins, or ingots.

Business Debt: Debt taken on by entrepreneurs to fund their business ventures, with varying terms and interest rates.

Business Insurance: Insurance for businesses to protect against financial losses, including property, liability, and business interruption coverage.

Capital Expenditure: Money spent on acquiring or upgrading physical assets with long-term value.

Capital Gains Tax: Tax levied on the profit from selling assets like stocks or real estate.

Capital Gains: Profit earned from the sale of assets like stocks or real estate.

Capital Gains: Profits earned from the sale of investments or assets.

Capital Loss: A financial loss resulting from the sale of an investment for less than its purchase price.

Capital Market: The financial market where stocks, bonds, and other long-term investments are bought and sold.

Capital: Money invested in a business or asset with the expectation of generating future income or profit.

Capitalization Rate (Cap Rate): A measure used to evaluate the potential return on a real estate investment.

Cash Flow: The movement of money into and out of an individual's accounts or a business.

Catch-Up Contributions: Higher annual contribution limits allowed for individuals aged 50 and older in retirement accounts.

Certificate of Deposit (CD): A time-bound savings deposit with a fixed interest rate.

Charitable Giving: Donating to qualified organizations, resulting in valuable tax deductions.

Charitable Lead Trust (CLT): A trust that provides income to a charitable organization for a defined period, after which the remaining assets pass to heirs, potentially with estate tax benefits.

Charitable Remainder Trust (CRT): A trust that provides income to beneficiaries for a specified period, with the remaining assets going to a charitable organization, potentially reducing capital gains taxes.

Charitable Trusts: Trusts facilitating charitable giving with potential tax benefits.

Collateral: An asset used to secure a loan, which the lender can seize if the borrower defaults.

Compound Annual Growth Rate (CAGR): The rate at which an investment grows annually to reach a certain end value.

Compound Interest: The interest earned on both the initial principal and the accumulated interest on a deposit or investment, leading to exponential growth over time.

Consumer Debt: Debt incurred for personal expenses, such as credit card balances, personal loans, and payday loans, often characterized by higher interest rates.

Consumer Price Index (CPI): A measure of the average change in prices paid by urban consumers for a basket of goods and services over time.

Cost of Living: The amount of money needed to maintain a certain standard of living.

Credit Card: A payment card that allows individuals to borrow money for purchases, subject to interest charges.

Credit Report: A detailed record of your credit history, including open and closed credit accounts, payment history, inquiries, and public records like bankruptcies.

Credit Score: A numerical representation of your creditworthiness, with higher scores indicating better creditworthiness and potentially more favorable lending terms.

Custodial Accounts (UGMA/UTMA): Accounts that allow parents or guardians to invest on behalf of a minor, with funds becoming the property of the minor upon reaching adulthood.

Cyber Insurance: Insurance that covers financial losses resulting from cyberattacks, data breaches, and other cyber threats.
Debit Card: A payment card that deducts funds directly from a checking account to pay for purchases.
Debt Consolidation: Combining multiple debts into a single loan, often with a lower interest rate, to simplify payments and reduce overall interest.
Debt: Money borrowed that must be repaid, often with interest.
Default: Failure to meet the terms and obligations of a loan or debt.
Defined Benefit Pension: A defined benefit pension is a retirement plan where an employer promises a specific retirement benefit based on factors like salary and years of service. The employer bears the investment risk.
Defined Contribution Plan: A defined contribution plan is a retirement plan where employees and/or employers contribute to individual accounts, with the retirement benefit depending on contributions and investment performance.
Depreciation: The decrease in the value of an asset over time due to wear and tear or obsolescence.
Disability Insurance: Coverage that replaces a portion of income if the policyholder is unable to work due to injury or illness.
Diversification: A strategy that involves spreading investments across different asset classes or types to reduce risk and potential losses.

Divestment: The process of selling an asset, business, or investment.
Dividend Yield: A measure of a company's annual dividend income relative to its share price.
Dividends: Payments made by corporations to their shareholders as a distribution of profits.
Donor-Advised Funds (DAFs): Charitable giving accounts that allow donors to contribute funds, receive immediate tax deductions, and recommend grants to charitable organizations.
Down Payment: A initial payment made when purchasing a big-ticket item, often associated with buying a home, that represents a percentage of the total purchase price.
Durable Power of Attorney: A legal document that allows an individual to appoint someone to manage their affairs in the event they become incapacitated.
Economic Downturns: Periods of economic decline characterized by reduced economic activity, job losses, and decreased consumer spending.
Educational Savings Plans: Plans like 529 plans and Coverdell Education Savings Accounts with tax advantages for education expenses.
Emergency Fund: A savings account specifically designated to cover unexpected expenses or emergencies, providing financial stability and peace of mind during crises.
Employment: Working for an employer in exchange for a salary or wages.
Envelope System: A cash-based budgeting method in which individuals allocate specific amounts of cash to different

spending categories and use physical envelopes to store the money.

Escrow Account: An account where funds are held by a third party until specified conditions are met.

Estate Planning: Estate planning involves preparing for the distribution of assets after one's passing, including creating wills, designating beneficiaries, and considering estate tax strategies.

Estate Tax: Tax on the estate of a deceased person before it is passed on to heirs.

Exchange-Traded Fund (ETF): A type of investment fund and exchange-traded product, with shares that are tradeable on a stock exchange.

Expenses: Regular financial outflows, including bills, groceries, rent or mortgage payments, and other costs.

Factor-Based Investing: Investment strategies that target specific factors associated with higher returns, such as value, momentum, and quality.

FHA Loan: A mortgage loan insured by the Federal Housing Administration (FHA) with lower down payment requirements and more flexible credit criteria.

FICO Score: A credit scoring system used by lenders to assess credit risk.

Financial Advisor: A professional who provides financial guidance and advice to individuals or organizations to help them achieve their financial goals and manage investments.

Financial Awareness: A state of understanding one's financial situation, achieved through budgeting, tracking expenses, and gaining insights into spending habits.

Financial Discipline: The practice of managing finances responsibly, adhering to budgeted spending limits, and making informed financial decisions.

Financial Education: Educating heirs about financial matters and responsible asset management.

Financial Freedom: The state of having sufficient assets and passive income streams to cover living expenses and pursue personal goals without being financially constrained by employment.

Financial Goals: Specific objectives related to personal finance, which guide financial decisions and actions. Goals can be short-term, mid-term, or long-term.

Financial Literacy: The knowledge and understanding of financial concepts, such as budgeting, investing, and managing debt.

Financial Management: The strategic management of one's financial resources to achieve financial goals and maintain financial stability.

Financial Milestones: Significant achievements in one's financial journey that mark progress toward long-term goals and financial security.

Financial Roadmap: A structured plan that guides an individual's financial decisions, ensuring that their spending aligns with their priorities and objectives.

Financial Stability: A state of financial well-being characterized by having adequate savings, manageable debt, and a safety net to handle unexpected expenses.

Financial Statement: A summary of an individual's or organization's financial transactions and financial position.

Financial Stress: Psychological stress resulting from financial challenges or worries about money.

Financial Well-Being: A state of financial health and security that allows individuals to meet their financial goals and enjoy peace of mind.

Fixed Expenses: Predictable, regular financial obligations that remain consistent over time, often associated with essential needs.

Fixed-Rate Mortgage: A type of mortgage in which the interest rate remains constant for the duration of the loan.

Foreclosure: The legal process by which a lender repossesses a property due to mortgage default.

Free Application for Federal Student Aid (FAFSA): A form that must be completed by students seeking federal financial aid for college, including grants, loans, and work-study programs.

Generation-Skipping Transfer (GST) Tax Planning: Strategies for transferring wealth to grandchildren or subsequent generations while minimizing gift and estate taxes.

Grantor: An individual or entity that establishes a trust.

Health Insurance: Coverage that pays for medical expenses, protecting against the financial burden of healthcare costs.

Home Equity Line of Credit (HELOC): A line of credit secured by the equity in one's home, which can be used for various expenses.

Home Equity: The difference between the market value of a home and the outstanding mortgage balance.
Homeowners Association (HOA) Fees: Regular fees paid by homeowners to cover the cost of maintaining common areas, amenities, and community services in a managed community.
Homeowners Insurance: Insurance that covers property damage, theft, and liability for homeowners.
Income Generation: The process of creating various streams of revenue to support one's financial needs and goals, often involving diversifying income sources.
Income Tax: Taxes imposed on earnings, including wages, salaries, business income, and investment income.
Income: Money earned from various sources, such as wages, salaries, investments, and rental income.
Individual Retirement Account (IRA): An individual retirement savings account that offers tax advantages for retirement savings, with traditional and Roth IRAs being common types.
Inflation: Inflation is the gradual increase in the prices of goods and services over time, eroding the purchasing power of money. It's an important consideration in retirement planning.
Inheritance Tax: Tax on the transfer of wealth from one generation to the next.
Inheritance: An inheritance refers to assets or wealth passed down to heirs or beneficiaries, which can increase retirement income.

Insurance: A contractual arrangement that provides financial protection or reimbursement against specific losses or unexpected events.

Intangible Asset: An asset that lacks physical substance, such as patents, copyrights, or trademarks.

Interest Rate: The percentage charged by a lender or earned by an investor on an amount of money, usually expressed as an annual percentage rate (APR).

Interest: Money earned from lending money or investing in interest-bearing assets like bonds or savings accounts.

Interest-Only Mortgage: A mortgage where the borrower pays only the interest for a specified initial period, after which they begin paying both principal and interest.

Investments: Allocating capital to assets like stocks, bonds, real estate, etc., to generate income or capital gains over time.

IRAs (Individual Retirement Accounts): IRAs are tax-advantaged retirement savings accounts that individuals can open and contribute to independently of employer-sponsored plans.

Irrevocable Trusts: Trusts that cannot be altered or revoked without beneficiary consent.

Jumbo Loan: A mortgage loan that exceeds the conforming loan limits set by Fannie Mae and Freddie Mac.

Liabilities: Debts or financial obligations that an individual owes to others.

Life Insurance: Protection that provides a financial safety net to beneficiaries in the event of the policyholder's death.

Liquidity Risk: The risk that an asset cannot be easily sold or converted into cash without a significant loss in value.
Liquidity: The ease with which an asset can be converted into cash without significant loss of value.
Living Trusts: Trusts created during one's lifetime that allow for asset management and control.
Long Position: Owning an asset, such as a stock or bond, with the expectation that it will increase in value.
Longevity: Longevity refers to the length of time people live, especially in the context of retirement planning. People are living longer, necessitating longer financial planning for retirement.
Long-Term Care Insurance: Long-term care insurance provides coverage for expenses associated with long-term care, such as nursing home care or in-home assistance, which may become necessary in retirement.
Long-Term Goals: Financial objectives that extend over many years, such as saving for retirement.
Medical Debt: Debt resulting from medical expenses, often due to unexpected healthcare costs, and may involve payment plans or financial assistance options.
Medicare: Medicare is a federal health insurance program for people aged 65 and older and some younger individuals with disabilities. It can be a significant part of retirement healthcare planning.
Mid-Term Goals: Financial objectives with a timeframe of a few years, such as saving for a car.

Mortgage Debt: A loan used to purchase real estate, typically a home, with typically lower interest rates compared to consumer debt.

Mortgage Rate: The interest rate charged on a mortgage loan.

Mortgage Refinancing: The process of replacing an existing mortgage with a new one, often to obtain better terms or lower interest rates.

Mortgage: A loan used to finance the purchase of a home or real estate, typically repaid over an extended period with interest.

Multi-Asset Investing: Combining various asset classes, factors, and strategies into a single investment vehicle.

Multigenerational Planning: Planning that extends beyond immediate beneficiaries to multiple generations.

Mutual Fund: An investment vehicle that pools money from multiple investors to purchase a diversified portfolio of stocks, bonds, or other securities.

Net Income: The amount of money an individual or business earns after deducting taxes and expenses.

Net Worth: The difference between an individual's assets and liabilities, representing their overall financial position.

Networking: Building and leveraging professional relationships to discover job opportunities.

Passive Income Streams: Sources of income that require minimal effort or active involvement, such as rental income, dividends, or interest from investments.

Penny Stocks: Low-priced stocks with a small market capitalization, often considered high-risk investments.

Personal Finance: The management of one's money and financial resources, including budgeting, saving, investing, and retirement planning.

Personal Loan: A loan for personal use, often unsecured and with a fixed interest rate.

Pet Insurance: Insurance covering veterinary expenses for pet illnesses or injuries.

Philanthropy and Giving: Incorporating charitable giving and philanthropy into legacy planning.

Portfolio Diversification: Portfolio diversification involves spreading investments across different asset classes to reduce risk. It's a key strategy in retirement planning.

Portfolio Manager: An individual or entity responsible for managing an investment portfolio on behalf of clients.

Portfolio Rebalancing: The process of adjusting the asset allocation in an investment portfolio to align with financial goals and risk tolerance.

Portfolio: A collection of investments, such as stocks, bonds, and mutual funds, held by an individual or entity.

Power of Attorney (POA): Legal authorization given to one person to act on behalf of another in financial and legal matters.

Principal: The initial amount of money invested or borrowed, before any interest or earnings are added.

Professional Guidance: Involvement of legal, financial, and tax professionals in estate planning.

Property Tax: Tax assessed on the value of real estate or other properties.

Protecting Your Finances: Safeguarding financial well-being through insurance, estate planning, and long-term financial security.

Qualified Charitable Distributions (QCDs): Distributions from an individual's IRA to a qualified charitable organization, which can satisfy required minimum distributions (RMDs) and exclude the distribution from taxable income.

Rebalancing: The process of adjusting the allocation of assets in a portfolio to maintain the desired asset mix and risk level.

Rental Income: Rental income is money received from owning and renting out real estate properties, which can be a source of retirement income for property owners.

Renters Insurance: Insurance for tenants that covers personal property and offers liability protection within a rented dwelling.

Retirement Budget: A retirement budget is a detailed financial plan that outlines expected expenses during retirement, including essentials like housing and healthcare, as well as discretionary spending.

Retirement Nest Egg: The accumulated savings and investments set aside to fund retirement and achieve financial independence.

Retirement: The point at which individuals choose to stop working and rely on savings, investments, and other income sources to support their lifestyle.

Risk Assessment: The evaluation of potential risks and their impact on financial decisions.

Risk Management: Strategies and techniques used to mitigate financial risks.
Risk Parity Strategy: A strategy that aims to achieve balanced risk across different asset classes.
Risk Premium: The potential return or compensation an investor expects for taking on additional risk.
Risk Tolerance: Risk tolerance refers to an individual's ability and willingness to withstand fluctuations and uncertainties in financial markets. It influences investment decisions and asset allocation.
Rollover IRA: An individual retirement account used to hold funds transferred from another retirement account.
Roth IRA Conversion: The process of converting funds from a traditional IRA to a Roth IRA, potentially providing tax-free withdrawals in retirement.
Roth IRA: An IRA that does not provide immediate tax deductions for contributions, but qualified withdrawals in retirement are entirely tax-free.
Sales Tax: Tax added to the purchase price of goods and services at the point of sale.
Self-Employment: Running a business or providing freelance services independently, often with greater control over earnings but also more risk.
Short Position: Borrowing an asset and selling it with the expectation of buying it back at a lower price.
Short-Term Goals: Financial objectives that are typically achievable within a year or less, such as paying off credit card debt.

Side Hustles: Additional income-generating activities pursued alongside a primary job.

Simplified Employee Pension (SEP) IRAs: Retirement plans designed for self-employed individuals and small business owners, allowing for tax-deductible contributions.

Snowball Method: A debt reduction strategy where you prioritize paying off the smallest debts first while making minimum payments on others to build motivation.

Social Security: Social Security is a government program that provides retirement benefits to eligible individuals based on their work history and contributions to the system.

Special Needs Trusts: Trusts providing for individuals with disabilities without affecting government assistance eligibility.

Standard & Poor's 500 (S&P 500): A stock market index that measures the performance of 500 of the largest companies listed on stock exchanges in the United States.

Staying Informed and Adapting: The importance of keeping up with financial news and being flexible in adjusting financial strategies as life circumstances change.

Stock: Ownership shares in a company, representing a claim on assets and earnings.

Student Loans: Loans that finance education expenses, available with various terms and interest rates, including federal and private student loans.

Succession Planning for Businesses: Planning for the transition of a business to the next generation or successor.

Supplemental Health Insurance: Supplemental health insurance covers healthcare expenses not covered by primary

health insurance plans, which can be important during retirement.
Tactical Asset Allocation: Actively adjusting the allocation of assets in response to changing market conditions.
Tangible Asset: An asset that has physical substance, such as real estate, vehicles, or machinery.
Tax Credits: Direct reductions in the amount of tax owed, often based on specific criteria like education expenses or having children.
Tax Deductions: Expenses or contributions that reduce taxable income, lowering the overall tax liability.
Tax Evasion: Illegal activities involving misrepresentation or illegal actions to evade taxes, subject to legal consequences.
Tax Filing Status: Designation that affects tax brackets and eligibility for certain deductions and credits, such as single, married filing jointly, or head of household.
Tax Planning: The strategic process of optimizing one's financial situation by minimizing tax liability within the bounds of tax laws.
Tax Professional: A qualified expert who provides guidance on tax-related matters and ensures compliance with tax laws.
Tax Shelter: A legal method or investment that reduces an individual's tax liability.
Tax Withholding: The process of deducting taxes from an individual's income or payments.
Tax-Advantaged Savings Accounts: Accounts like Health Savings Accounts (HSAs) and Flexible Spending Accounts (FSAs) that offer pre-tax benefits.

Tax-Deferred Retirement Accounts: Accounts like 401(k)s or IRAs that allow contributions to grow tax-free until retirement.

Tax-Efficient Investment Portfolio: Constructing a portfolio that minimizes taxable events through strategies like tax-efficient fund selection, tax-loss harvesting, and efficient asset location.

Tax-Loss Harvesting: Selling investments that have declined in value to offset capital gains for tax purposes.

Time Horizon: The length of time an individual expects to hold an investment before needing access to the funds.

Traditional IRA: An IRA where contributions may be tax-deductible, and earnings grow tax-deferred until withdrawal in retirement.

Travel Insurance: Coverage for unexpected events during travel, such as trip cancellations, medical emergencies, or delays.

Trustee: An individual or entity responsible for managing assets held in a trust on behalf of beneficiaries.

Trusts: Legal arrangements allowing the transfer of assets to a trustee who manages and distributes them according to specified terms.

Umbrella Insurance: Liability insurance that provides additional coverage beyond the limits of other policies.

Unemployment Benefits: Financial assistance provided to individuals who have lost their jobs, typically paid by government programs.

Unsecured Debt: Debt that is not backed by collateral or assets and relies on the borrower's creditworthiness.

USDA Loan: A mortgage loan designed for eligible rural and suburban homebuyers, offering competitive terms and low down payment requirements.
VA Loan: A mortgage loan available to eligible veterans, service members, and their families, often with favorable terms such as 100% financing.
Variable Expenses: Discretionary or fluctuating expenses, such as groceries, entertainment, and dining out, which may change from month to month.
Wealth Building: The process of accumulating assets and financial resources over time to achieve financial stability and a comfortable future.
Wills: Legal documents outlining asset distribution and guardianship arrangements after the death of the individual.
Windfalls and Bonuses: Unexpected income sources like tax refunds or work bonuses that can be directed toward debt payoff.
Yield: The income generated by an investment, typically expressed as a percentage of its current value.

B. Recommended Books and Resources

General Personal Finance:

1. "The Total Money Makeover" by Dave Ramsey

2. "Your Money or Your Life" by Vicki Robin and Joe Dominguez

3. "Rich Dad Poor Dad" by Robert Kiyosaki

4. "The Millionaire Next Door" by Thomas J. Stanley and William D. Danko

5. "I Will Teach You to Be Rich" by Ramit Sethi

Investing:

6. "The Intelligent Investor" by Benjamin Graham

7. "A Random Walk Down Wall Street" by Burton G. Malkiel

8. "One Up On Wall Street" by Peter Lynch

9. "The Little Book of Common Sense Investing" by John C. Bogle

10. "The Essays of Warren Buffett" edited by Lawrence A. Cunningham

Budgeting and Saving:

11. "Broke Millennial" by Erin Lowry

12. "You Need a Budget" by Jesse Mecham

13. "The Richest Man in Babylon" by George S. Clason

14. "Automatic Millionaire" by David Bach

15. "Zero Down Your Debt" by Holly Porter Johnson and Greg Johnson

Financial Independence and Early Retirement (FIRE):

16. "Early Retirement Extreme" by Jacob Lund Fisker

17. "The Simple Path to Wealth" by J.L. Collins

18. "Quit Like a Millionaire" by Kristy Shen and Bryce Leung

19. "Financial Freedom: A Proven Path to All the Money You Will Ever Need" by Grant Sabatier

20. "Playing with FIRE" by Scott Rieckens

Real Estate and Real Estate Investing:

21. "Rich Dad's Guide to Investing in Real Estate" by Robert Kiyosaki

22. "Real Estate Investing for Dummies" by Eric Tyson and Robert S. Griswold

23. "The Book on Rental Property Investing" by Brandon Turner

24. "Real Estate Investing: Market Analysis, Valuation Techniques, and Risk Management" by David M. Geltner and Norman G. Miller

25. "Real Estate Investing: Market Analysis, Valuation Techniques, and Risk Management" by David M. Geltner and Norman G. Miller

Behavioral Finance and Psychology:

26. "Nudge: Improving Decisions About Health, Wealth, and Happiness" by Richard H. Thaler and Cass R. Sunstein

27. "Thinking, Fast and Slow" by Daniel Kahneman

28. "Why Smart People Make Big Money Mistakes and How to Correct Them" by Gary Belsky and Thomas Gilovich

29. "The Behavior Gap" by Carl Richards

30. "The Psychology of Money" by Morgan Housel

Retirement Planning:

31. "How to Retire Happy, Wild, and Free" by Ernie J. Zelinski

32. "Retire Inspired: It's Not an Age, It's a Financial Number" by Chris Hogan

33. "The Bogleheads' Guide to Retirement Planning" by Taylor Larimore, Mel Lindauer, and Richard A. Ferri

34. "Get What's Yours: The Secrets to Maxing Out Your Social Security" by Laurence J. Kotlikoff, Philip Moeller, and Paul Solman

35. "The Retirement Savings Time Bomb... and How to Defuse It" by Ed Slott

Debt Management:

36. "The Total Money Makeover" by Dave Ramsey (also listed under general personal finance)

37. "Debt-Free Forever: Take Control of Your Money and Your Life" by Gail Vaz-Oxlade

38. "The Debt-Free Millionaire: Winning Strategies to Creating Great Credit and Retiring Rich" by Anthony Manganiello

39. "Debt: The First 5,000 Years" by David Graeber

40. "Paying the Price: College Costs, Financial Aid, and the Betrayal of the American Dream" by Sara Goldrick-Rab

Estate Planning and Wills:

41. "Get It Together: Organize Your Records So Your Family Won't Have To" by Melanie Cullen and Shae Irving

42. "Estate Planning Basics" by Denis Clifford

43. "The Four Pillars of Investing: Lessons for Building a Winning Portfolio" by William J. Bernstein

44. "The Inheritance: A Family on the Front Lines of the Battle Against Alzheimer's Disease" by Niki Kapsambelis

45. "Beyond the Grave, Revised and Updated Edition: The Right Way and the Wrong Way of Leaving Money to Your Children (and Others)" by Gerald M. Condon and Jeffrey L. Condon

Personal Finance for Millennials and Young Adults:

46. "Broke Millennial" by Erin Lowry (also listed under budgeting and saving)

47. "The Broke and Beautiful Life" by Stefanie O'Connell

48. "The Financial Diet: A Total Beginner's Guide to Getting Good with Money" by Chelsea Fagan

49. "Get a Financial Life: Personal Finance in Your Twenties and Thirties" by Beth Kobliner

50. "Invested: How Warren Buffett and Charlie Munger Taught Me to Master My Mind, My Emotions, and My Money (with a Little Help from My Dad)" by Danielle Town

Women and Finance:

51. "Women and Money: Owning the Power to Control Your Destiny" by Suze Orman

52. "Smart Women Finish Rich: 9 Steps to Achieving Financial Security and Funding Your Dreams" by David Bach

53. "The Feminist Financial Handbook: A Modern Woman's Guide to a Wealthy Life" by Brynne Conroy

54. "When She Makes More: 10 Rules for Breadwinning Women" by Farnoosh Torabi

55. "Girl, Get Your Money Straight!" by Glinda Bridgforth and Gail Perry-Mason

Books for Entrepreneurs:

56. "The Lean Startup" by Eric Ries

57. "Rich Dad's Cashflow Quadrant" by Robert Kiyosaki

58. "The E-Myth Revisited: Why Most Small Businesses Don't Work and What to Do About It" by Michael E. Gerber

59. "Good to Great: Why Some Companies Make the Leap... and Others Don't" by Jim Collins

60. "The One-Person Business" by Elaine Pofeldt

Books on Mindset and Success:

61. "Mindset: The New Psychology of Success" by Carol S. Dweck

62. "The Success Principles: How to Get from Where You Are to Where You Want to Be" by Jack Canfield

63. "Grit: The Power of Passion and Perseverance" by Angela Duckworth

64. "The Power of Habit: Why We Do What We Do in Life and Business" by Charles Duhigg

65. "Atomic Habits: An Easy & Proven Way to Build Good Habits & Break Bad Ones" by James Clear

Books for Financial Advisors:

66. "The Million-Dollar Financial Services Practice: A Proven System for Becoming a Top Producer" by David J. Mullen Jr.

67. "The Millionaire Advisor: Powerful Lessons in Personal Finance" by Russell Walker

68. "The Wealthy Advisor: The High-Net-Worth Planning Techniques of the Pros" by Russell L. Chipps

69. "The Financial Advisor's Guide to Excellence: Becoming a World-Class Advisor" by Howard M. Guttman

70. "Becoming a Wealth Strategist: Advanced Techniques to Make a Significant Difference in Your Financial Practice" by Peter Christman and Mark Peabody

Budgeting and Expense Tracking:

1. **Mint:** A free budgeting app that helps you track your spending, set financial goals, and monitor your accounts in one place.

2. **Personal Capital:** Offers budgeting tools and investment tracking, making it easier to manage your entire financial life.

3. **YNAB (You Need a Budget):** A budgeting app that focuses on allocating your income to specific categories, helping you gain better control over your spending.

Investment Platforms and Tools:

4. **Robinhood:** A commission-free trading platform that allows you to invest in stocks, ETFs, options, and cryptocurrencies.

5. **E*TRADE:** A comprehensive online brokerage platform with a wide range of investment options and educational resources.

6. **Vanguard:** Known for its low-cost index funds and ETFs, Vanguard offers a user-friendly platform for DIY investors.

7. **Morningstar:** Provides investment research, including mutual fund and ETF analysis, portfolio tracking, and financial news.

8. **StockCharts:** Offers technical analysis tools for investors interested in charting and analyzing stock market trends.

Retirement Planning and Calculators:

9. **Fidelity Retirement Planner:** Provides retirement planning tools, calculators, and educational content to help you set and achieve your retirement goals.

10. **Social Security Administration:** Offers calculators and resources to help you estimate your Social Security benefits and make informed decisions about retirement.

Financial Education and Learning:

11. **Investopedia:** A comprehensive resource for financial education, offering articles, tutorials, and a financial dictionary.

12. **Khan Academy:** Provides free online courses on a wide range of financial topics, including investing, retirement, and personal finance.

13. **Coursera and edX:** Offer online courses from top universities and institutions, covering various financial subjects.

Credit Monitoring and Reporting:

14. **Credit Karma:** Allows you to monitor your credit scores and provides personalized recommendations to improve your credit health.

15. **AnnualCreditReport.com:** Provides access to your free credit reports from all three major credit bureaus (Equifax, Experian, and TransUnion) once a year.

Tax Preparation:

16. **TurboTax:** A popular tax preparation software that guides you through the tax-filing process and maximizes potential deductions.

17. **H&R Block:** Offers tax preparation software and in-person tax services, including professional advice and assistance.

Robo-Advisors:

18. **Wealthfront:** A robo-advisor that offers automated, low-cost investment management with features like tax-loss harvesting.

19. **Betterment:** Provides a user-friendly platform for automated investing, along with personalized financial advice.

Real Estate and Homebuying:

20. **Zillow:** A real estate website that offers information on homes for sale, rental listings, and home value estimates.

21. **Redfin:** A real estate brokerage platform that provides home-buying and selling services, including tools to estimate home values.

Financial News and Research:

22. **Bloomberg:** Offers a wide range of financial news, market data, and analysis on global financial markets.

23. **CNBC:** Provides real-time financial news, market updates, and expert analysis on business and finance.

24. **The Wall Street Journal:** A respected source of business and financial news, with in-depth coverage of global markets.

Peer-to-Peer Lending:

25. **LendingClub:** Allows you to invest in personal loans and potentially earn interest income.

26. **Prosper:** Offers a similar peer-to-peer lending platform, connecting borrowers and investors.

Cryptocurrency and Blockchain:

27. **Coinbase:** A popular platform for buying, selling, and storing cryptocurrencies like Bitcoin and Ethereum.

28. **Binance:** A cryptocurrency exchange that offers a wide range of digital assets for trading.